自然建造
ARCHITECTURE
CHINA
AWARD

ARCHITECTURE
CHINA

Trophy Design by Qin Xiaowan and Li Hongkai

CONTENTS

Exploration Award for Young Architects

Special Project Award

2020 Architecture China Award

Award Concept

The theme of the 2020 Architecture China Award, *Building with Nature*, looks at returning to the path of nature in contemporary Chinese architecture, or similar related concepts. Proposed by architects Wang Shu and Lu Wenyu, the theme is well placed in today's over-industrialized context and explores the poetry behind the constructions of the qualifying nominees.

The poetry in "building with nature" is created through a blend of nature, architecture, and the city. Building with Nature – 2020 Architecture China Award (the Award) acknowledges (and in that encourages) contemporary manifestations of the "building with nature" concept, while also advocating learning from the countryside—not only on architecture and methods of construction, but also on promoting a way of life that is harmonious with nature. Alongside the exploration and use of traditional materials and construction systems, the Award also promotes the integration of modern technologies. Future architecture, as envisioned based on the theme of this 2020 Architecture China Award, will reconnect the city, architecture, and nature with poetry, painting new ways of construction that are inseparable, difficult to classify, and dense.

Introduction of Award

In 2016, Wang Shu served as jury chairman for the 4th China Architecture Media Awards sponsored by Nanfang Media Group and *Southern Metropolis Daily*, and had proposed "building with nature" as a selection criterion for the award. In 2019, the concept was adopted by the English-language architecture journal, *Architecture China*, as a theme to shape the 2020 Architecture China Award. As "building with nature" is the fundamental requisite and core idea of the Award, it was accordingly named the same. *Architecture China* is the first global English-language publication focusing on the development of architectural design in contemporary China, and organizer of the 2020 Architecture China Award.

There are four categories in the Award: Architecture China Award in Practice, Exploration Award in Technology, Exploration Award for Young Architects, and Special Project Award, and the review system models the process in major international architecture awards—establish committees for organization, nomination, and evaluation.

Award recipients will be selected every two years; in addition to the nominations by the evaluation and nomination committees, both Chinese and foreign architects who have completed two or more high-level works in the Chinese mainland, Taiwan, and Hong Kong can also apply for consideration.

Evaluation Committee

Wang Shu (chair of the Evaluation Committee)
2012 laureate, Pritzker Architecture Prize
Jury, Pritzker Architecture Prize
Professor and Head, Architecture School, China Academy of Art

Cui Kai
Honorary President and Chief Architect, China Architecture Design & Research Group
Academician, Chinese Academy of Engineering

Yung Ho Chang
Former jury, Pritzker Architecture Prize
Principal, Atelier FCJZ

Li Xiangning
Professor and Dean, College of Architecture and Urban Planning, Tongji University

Ge Ming
Professor and Deputy Dean, School of Architecture, Southeast University

Wang Lu
Professor, School of Architecture, Tsinghua University

Aric Chen
Independent curator
Professor, College of Design and Innovation, Tongji University

Ching-Yueh Roan
Professor, Yuan Ze University

Benedetta Tagliabue
Jury, Pritzker Architecture Prize
Principal, Miralles Tagliabue EMBT

Iwan Baan
Architectural photographer

Philip Ursprung
Professor and Chair of the History of Art and Architecture, ETH Zürich

自然建造
ARCHITECTURE CHINA AWARD

Award Structure

Architecture China Award in Practice

Architecture China Award in Practice is the highest-ranking category in the 2020 Architecture China Award. It honors an architect who has demonstrated "building with nature" or related concepts in his or her long-term architectural practice and requires that the architect has completed three or more high-quality works in the past ten years.

Three finalists are selected, among which a single architect is granted the Practical Achievement Award, with a cash prize of 100,000 RMB. Two other finalists are granted Shortlisted awards.

Exploration Award in Technology

Exploration Award in Technology focuses on projects with a humanistic spirit and which display continuous innovation with architectural technologies through two or more high-quality works created in recent years. This award also encourages cross-professional and cross-disciplinary exploration.

Three finalists are selected, of which one is awarded the Technology Exploration Award, with a cash prize of 50,000 RMB. The remaining two finalists are granted Shortlisted awards.

Exploration Award for Young Architects

Exploration Award for Young Architects is granted to young architects under the age of forty-five who have completed two or more high-quality works in recent years. It aims to show professional recognition while encouraging the experimental spirit of young architects.

Six finalists are selected, of which three are granted the Exploration Award for Young Architects, with a cash prize of 30,000 RMB each. The remaining three finalists are granted Shortlisted awards.

Special Project Award

The special Project Award is given to high-quality architectural works completed in recent years that embody the *Building with Nature* concept, or similar concepts. The recipients are nominated and selected by the members of the jury.

Organizing Committee

Nan Dao
Director, *Southern Metropolis Daily*

Lu Wenyu
Professor, Architecture School, China Academy of Art

Li Xiangning
Professor and Dean, College of Architecture and Urban Planning, Tongji University

Ge Ming
Professor and Deputy Dean, School of Architecture, Southeast University

Li Hui
Founder, Shanghai Fengyuzhu Culture Technology Co., Ltd.

Chief Partner

Shanghai Fengyuzhu Culture Technology Co., Ltd.

Pre-selection and final jury meeting of Building with Nature – 2020 Architecture China Award

October 19, 2019

Award Launch

The Architecture China Award was launched at the Architectural Model Museum in Shanghai. The launch ceremony was hosted by jury member Li Xiangning and launch addresses were delivered by Wang Shu, chair of the evaluation committee, jury members Ge Ming and Yung Ho Chang, and Li Hui, chairman of Shanghai Fengyuzhu Culture Technology Co., Ltd. the main sponsor of the award.

December 28, 2019

Pre-selection

Seven jury members partook in the pre-selection process at the Xiangshan campus of the China Academy of Art in Hangzhou, China. This first Architecture China Award received a total of 176 applications, among which there were 138 valid documents. The 138 valid documents included twenty-three applications for Architecture China Award in Practice, twenty-two applications for Exploration Award in Technology, and seventy-one applications for Exploration Award for Young Architects.

August 20, 2020

Final Jury Meeting

Due to COVID-19, the final jury meeting was held both online and offline. Jury members who were from different countries and time zones met online with the jury members in China. The meeting was hosted at the Xiangshan Campus of the China Academy of Art. The jury members discussed the candidates and the shortlisted projects in depth and expressed their recognition and appreciation. Once the voting for each category ended, the final jury meeting completed the closing review of the Architecture China Award in Practice, the Exploration Award in Technology, and the Exploration Award for Young Architects, as well as the Special Project Award.

Jury

Wang Shu (Chair)

Cui Kai

Yung Ho Chang

Li Xiangning

Ge Ming

Wang Lu

Aric Chen

Benedetta Tagliabue

Iwan Baan

Philip Ursprung

Wang Shu

"As the chair of the evaluation committee, I'm very happy to see that everyone has enjoyed the process. I think we had a great discussion today. The Building with Nature – 2020 Architecture China Award shows that we share similar sentiments about the way architecture should and will develop in the future. It's really nice that we found a lot of diversity and variety in architecture today. I think this is very good for Chinese architecture. This year, the majority of the winners are very young and this gives us more expectations about the future."

Cui Kai

"I'm very glad to see so many young architects and their wonderful works. I'm looking forward to seeing more of them achieve the completion of great projects. I also hope this award will perhaps lead the development of contemporary Chinese architecture in the future."

Yung Ho Chang

"I think the diversity of the award-winning projects sends a very positive message to architects, especially young architects. It tells the young people that they should pursue their own ideas and ideals because you never know which ideas will actually be developed and accepted by the field, as well as by the society. I think right now, it's a terrible moment for the world, and hopefully, with these awards, we're also sending a humanistic signal to the world."

Li Xiangning

"This is a very special moment in time. Even though the world battles the COVID-19 pandemic and globalization is cracking down, we still believe that exchange and communications among different cultures are important in every corner of the world. With this award, we hope to witness the growth of contemporary Chinese architecture in the future."

Ge Ming

"It's my great pleasure to join the jury. For me, 'building with nature' is an idea for architecture, as well as an attitude about architecture, and it also provides a possibility for architects to think and develop design method in their practice."

Wang Lu

"I think the Architecture China Award is a very high-quality and professional award. All the projects are very impressive. I hope, in the future, it will support more architects, especially the young generation."

Aric Chen

"It is really great to be part of this jury. It was a real gift to see so many works that I wasn't aware of and I'm now definitely more interested and eager to see more of such works in the future. I look forward to seeing more works by female architects, architects from outside of the major centers, and more projects by non-Chinese architects."

Benedetta Tagliabue

"It was really enjoyable to be part of this jury. Despite the physical distance, it's really beautiful to go through the ideas, projects, and think about where architecture is going. It was also very enjoyable because we studied the projects and discovered these fantastic architectures with the real desire toward being the best. This was the best surprise for me. Through this jury, there will be the possibility to make these fantastic works and experiments in China today more well-known to the rest of the world."

Iwan Baan

"I was really surprised with the variety of the works and especially, by a couple of fresh, new projects. It's really nice to see what is being designed in China now."

Philip Ursprung

"It's been an honor to be on this jury. I'm very impressed by the high quality and originality of the projects. I think from an international point of view, it's good that we're reviewing architecture in China instead of Chinese architecture. For the next round, it will be perhaps good to see more female architects."

Photography:
Aric Chen © Mark Cocksedge
Iwan Baan © Jonas Eriksson
Philip Ursprung © Katalin Deér

Natural Construction

Wang Shu
Chair of the Evaluation Committee, Architecture China Award
Jury member of the Pritzker Architecture Prize
Professor and Head of the Architecture School, China Academy of Art

As I have said before, I only explore houses, not architecture; once I even proposed "Chinese Houses" as the name for an exhibition.

I have said that, to me, a house is amateur architecture, and I refer specifically to the seemingly small, yet growing, bottom-up construction practice. It is either deemed traditional, or from the perspective of modern society, as a violation of the rules. It is beyond the scope of the ordinary schools of architecture.

Compared to the artificial, large-scale constructions in the name of modern architecture, the concept of the house points to a great variety of things. However, they all share a common characteristic: the state of being weak in the face of nature—of being non-monumental, and therefore, always being easy to integrate. It does not seek to express anything but the construction itself, while its vigorous integration method grants a powerful presence that cannot be ignored.

In 2000, at the West Lake International Sculpture Exhibition in Hangzhou's Taiziwan Park, I created the first prototype of such a house by reusing soil excavated from the foundation pits dug for the works of the other sculptors; I also used small blue tiles left over during the demolition of residences on Hangzhou's Hefang Street. For the first time, my wife Lu Wenyu and I made rammed earth for construction with our own hands. The finalized work looked small, with only two rammed earth walls, each the height of a person, and a blue tiled path running through them, but it provided visitors with a fresh experience of walking, watching, sitting, and lying down. To keep with the practice of giving a traditional residence a local name, I named this house Wall Gate. After the four-month-long exhibition ended, the house was demolished by the park administration, claiming it damaged the environment. Interestingly, other sculptures made of stainless steel, bronze, concrete, fiberglass, and plastic were preserved in an effort to beautify the environment.

At the 2001 West Lake International Sculpture Exhibition on Guishan Mountain in Hangzhou, I created a second prototype of this construction concept using 4,000 gray bricks from nearby Suzhou. Two equally sized walls—one standing and one lying down—were placed on-site, with the standing one acting as a wall and window, and the reclined one serving as a table and chair. Fortunately, this piece has survived to this day in the woods on the edge of Guishan Mountain, facing an area of the city's famous West Lake.

In 2006, during the planning and construction of the first Chinese Pavilion at the Venice Architecture Biennale, I showcased this concept directly through the Tile Garden.

Making Wall Gate, *The Beginning of Design*
used with permission

Wall Gate, *The Beginning of Design*
used with permission

Together with three craftsmen and six students, Lu Wenyu and I built the 800-square-meter house in thirteen days using 60,000 small blue tiles salvaged from demolished houses in rural Zhejiang Province and 5,000 bamboo sticks as the two main materials. The project brought to the fore this question: Is large-scale urbanization the only way forward for China's cities and villages?

In 2007, we completed the second phase of the China Academy of Art Xiangshan Campus, which was based on this construction concept, and which is also the largest group of houses ever built by Amateur Architecture Studio. For this project, more than 7 million old bricks, tiles, and stones were salvaged from the demolition sites of traditional residences across Zhejiang Province. This is not just a cluster of houses, nor a mere experiment in new teaching methods and the use of space in university education; it's not just a new experience of the human body's tactile sensations at the intersection of natural and manufactured places, nor simply a school campus; it's also not just a set of poems composed of materials, patterns, and movements in harmony with the natural landscape—it's a prototype for urban architecture that both continues tradition and looks to the future.

In 2009, I introduced the concept of "building with nature," for the first time, into the syllabus of the fourth-grade architectural design course at the Architecture Department of the China Academy of Art. The teaching site sat at the foot of Wushan Mountain in downtown Hangzhou, amid the shattered bricks and tiles of the century-old residences on Shiwukui Lane, which were being demolished and rebuilt. Among the ruins, was a house I discovered in 2000 when I taught my first students from the China Academy of Art. It was the classic archetype of what I call the "Chinese House." Wushan was the more urban of villages in the historical district, in which all sorts of spontaneous bottom-up constructions took place. What I remember most vividly was their endless number of unexpected details. The most impressive building was a small two-story structure on the forest hillside. Its basic language was derived from the traditional Chuan-Dou timber structures of Zhejiang residences, with a typical gable roof and two rooms. A remarkable aspect of Chinese architectural tradition is that such a house-type can be described such that anyone familiar with its construction rules, even an illiterate craftsman, can recognize exactly what one is talking about, without the need to draw a picture. The extraordinary thing about this little structure was that since 2000, it had evolved into a different building entirely. Now, its façade was made up of a multitude of collected ready-made building parts for houses, including dozens of windows of different sizes and similar

Tile Garden © Forgemind ArchiMedia (licensed under CC BY 2.0)

shapes—square or rectangular—assembled in succession. To distinguish it from the famous "ribbon windows" of Le Corbusier, I dubbed this application "climbing windows," and I later used the technique in designing the second phase of Xiangshan Campus. In addition to the windows, there was even a wooden chair directly embedded into the wall as part of the façade. The house was elevated a little above Shiwukui Lane and I remember telling the students that this small house would be to the future of contemporary Chinese architecture—what Marcel Duchamp's *Fountain* is to contemporary Western art.

In Chinese tradition, the concept of a house includes a special meaning that I believe is best represented by Ni Zan's painting *The Rongxi Studio*.

A seemingly fragile house such as this is always easier to blend into a pre-existing urban or rural community. It, therefore, naturally stands on the side of diversity; on the side of the seemingly trivial things in life, and on the side of reality.

If I have to define architecture again, I would repeat what I had said before long ago: it is not the pavilion in Ni Zan's painting that represents architecture, but all the elements together in the composition, constituting a concept that I call "Chinese House," where the general understanding of architecture makes up only a part. What is more important is the realization that houses don't exist by themselves—they are part of an existing natural world, so they have to be carefully integrated. This integration process always begins in one place, and little by little, grows into a whole, relying on the body's experience of materials, constituting an extremely thorough construction process at its essence. This concept gives more value to the naturalness of the building process and the degree to which it harms nature and the existing environment. This authenticity far exceeds any fabricated perceptions of so-called architecture.

It is in this construction process that an architect becomes aware of the existence of two completely different kinds of modern architecture: one is anti-historical, pretending that nothing else in the world exists, embarking entirely from abstract concepts to create highly engineered pseudo-landmarks that often show-off technology and are enormous in volume, while simultaneously believing in supposed planning, always chasing after trends. The other, is the realization that any construction practice needs to take into account the existing surroundings, and that in the end, naturalness constitutes the bottom line. Respect for what already exists is the defining attitude. This construction practice always starts from the

Tile Garden © Forgemind ArchiMedia (licensed under CC BY 2.0)

Xiangshan Campus © CC BY-NC-SA 2.0

surrounding environment and the materials at hand. This kind of modesty allows the house to be part of the environment and not a subject itself, causing the house to be generally smaller in size, or to actively disintegrate into smaller pieces, while actively fusing with the diverse existing world. The builder of such a house is always suspicious of any planning, but acts more like a philosophical craftsperson who distances self from whatever is popular, inherently favoring natural materials, even if that person has to coexist with powerful, modern, manufactured materials and construction systems, and even if that person has to continuously struggle with complex and difficult situations.

Oftentimes, this concept of a house—especially the way it approaches materials and construction—is more akin to transforming an old building than building a new one. In other words, the new house is planned and built as if it was a renovation of an aged building, making it both new and old at the same time. This naturally resolves the conflict between tradition and modernity, and between heritage and innovation, and in this dissolution process, something new is constantly created.

For this attitude, which emphasizes the construction concept, the building's form is crucial, but not the most important factor. What is important is the state and the atmosphere of an accessible scene, as well as the hidden logic that upholds it all.

This definition of a house is based on the process of building with nature, which is born out of the clash between the unique Chinese cultural background and reality. However, the attitudes and practical skills it contains, and the problems it faces are the same as anywhere else in the world.

This concept of "building with nature" defines another kind of architecture. It is a method that begins with the simple and moves toward the complex; a method that I would describe as placing an emphasis on "seeing a world in a grain of sand" at all times. But it is also a somewhat hidden and rugged path back to nature; it is about a different kind of future.

Stones of China: Remarks on the Architecture China Award

Philip Ursprung
Professor and Chair of the History of Art and Architecture, ETH Zürich

Chinese Lingbi scholar's stone on the desk of Philip Ursprung, Zürich Switzerland
© Philip Ursprung

During the lockdown in Switzerland in spring 2020, when the borders were closed and movement became restricted to the immediate neighborhood, I sometimes looked at the Chinese scholar's rock that I keep near my desk. It is a gray-black Lingbi stone on a wooden base; I traveled along its miniature landscape in my imagination. Sitting in my armchair, I passed canyons and valleys, bridges, peaks, and plains. I imagined how the surface of the rock was formed by water and erosion over thousands of years and I wondered who might have found the rock, removed it—perhaps from the bottom of a lake—and placed it on a finely carved wooden pedestal.

For me, a scholar's rock is more than a decorative object. It resembles a lens, which helps to perceive topics in a new light and at the same time, connects different topics; it inspires to mediate the relation between the natural and the artificial, the human and the non-human, and to reflect on the interaction between humans and the geological climate. These musings not only confronted my thoughts with the reality of the times, they also form some of the key issues in the Anthropocene. The scholar's rock thus functions like an emblem for the Anthropocene, which describes the belief that we are living in a geological age induced by humans, or more precisely, by human societies that brought forward industrialization, and thereby, climate change, global warming, and the mass extinction of animals and plants. The Anthropocene is not merely a theory, but possibly the biggest danger we are facing, forming a horizon for politics, science, the arts, and even critical discourse.

Multifunction Hall and Waterfall Pavilion in Qinglongshan Park by Atelier XÜK © Xu Yifei

Architecture and Anthropocene

Interestingly, the Anthropocene has so far only vaguely affected architectural discourse, which still follows traditional, binary ideas of nature versus culture, or countryside versus city, and which still adheres to notions of urban growth and globalization. However, I find the theory of Anthropocene, which has been present for about a decade, more appropriate to address the urgent challenges of our times than the earlier concept of globalization. While globalization is about economy, the Anthropocene is about ecology. While globalization is driven by the centers of finance and trade and is seen from the perspective of power, the Anthropocene brings into light the perspective of the powerless. It gives voice to those who suffer from the dark side of industrialization and those most threatened by environmental disasters—not only humans, but also animals, plants, and inanimate matter. In the Anthropocene discourse, animals, plants, bacteria, viruses, and even rocks, clouds, and water have a right to be heard. The difference between the animated and the non-animated, between what is alive and what is not alive becomes unclear.

In summer 2020, I studied the projects shortlisted for the Building with Nature – 2020 Architecture China Award. Travel to China was still restricted. I had to rely on documents and on my memory of earlier trips to China. Again, I looked at the scholar's rock and again, I thought about the Anthropocene and the shifting relation between the human and the non-human. A common denominator of the buildings proposed for the Award is their porosity, in other words, the permeability between outside and inside. I found, in these works, many of the walls don't separate spaces, but connect them. I was struck by the passageways, stairs, and ramps that link the environment and the building, allowing one to move easily between different levels. Another common denominator is the strong relation of the buildings to the terrain. They seem to sit firmly on the ground, following the laws of gravity. The attachment to the earth is also manifested in the materials used—from rocks, bricks, and tiles, to bamboo and wood, as well as the gray, brown, black, and yellow colors that predominate. A third common denominator is the mediation between human and the non-human scale, for instance, the connection between the buildings and a mountain range, or a river, the dunes, the shore, or other large infrastructure projects.

1. West Village by Jiakun Architects © Arch-Exist
2. Longfu Life Experience Center by LUO Studio © Jin Weiqi

In China—like in other industrialized areas of the world—in villages, small towns, and the countryside away from the urban centers toward the outskirts of cities, a general trend is evident. Pollution, high costs, and traffic jams make life in the city less desirable than it was a decade ago, but this does not mean that that the flow of people, capital, energy, food, and materials toward the urban centers has stopped. And in the vacuum in the rural and provincial areas created by the urban pull since the 1980s, new possibilities for architecture are offered. China is not the only place where this shift is taking place, but its situation is exemplary. There is much political will and economic means to reduce the gap between the urban centers and the countryside. These dynamics result in ample opportunities for privately run small architecture firms, and committed private and public clients to propose architecture experiments and innovations which would be impossible on a larger scale. The fruits of this engagement are now visible. They bear lessons for architecture far beyond the borders of China.

Examples

A project that is emblematic for the mediation between the human scale and the urban scale is Liu Jiakun's West Village in Chengdu. With its intersection of commercial and public, and individual and collective spaces, labor and leisure, and natural and artificial environments, the West Village forms a microcosm. It resembles an architectural model of a way to live. The only comparable project with regard to scale is the SESC Pompéia by Lina Bo Bardo in São Paulo (1982), a factory that was turned into a community center. West Village demonstrates that nature and the city cannot be radically separated. It takes urbanization for granted and does not try to escape the reality—both positive and negative—of the dense city. Its message: architecture is about connection, not about separation, about proximity not distance, and about access, not exclusivity.

More than a third of the global carbon emissions are produced by the building and construction industry. Research in optimizing materials and construction techniques is, therefore, a crucial component in the discussion of the Anthropocene and global warming. Luo Yujie's Longfu Life Experience Center in Puyang (2018), a temporary structure for a real estate sales center, is an example of a sustainable construction. The project is striking because it goes way beyond being a solution to a given problem. It gives sustainability a face, so to speak, providing an aesthetic character to the ecological.

Lounge houses by Atelier Sounding Architecture
© Atelier Sounding Architecture

Rong Garden by Yinyuan Studio
© Wang Baozhen

Philip F. Yuan's (Archi-Union Architects) project In Bamboo in Chongzhou combines the aesthetics of ecology with the aesthetics of digital fabrication. A rural community center combing spaces of education and leisure, it is symbolic for the reactivation of the countryside. Local, traditional handicraft and high-tech construction technology combined in this project, which mediates between the pre-industrial past and the post-industrial present, and between a rural and an urban lifestyle. A new typology—a moebius-shaped roof—is invented to connect the city dweller with the rural inhabitant.

Wang Baozhen's (Yinyuan Studio) Rong Garden in Guanxi Province (2017) goes far in connecting the urban with the rural. The project developed gradually over ten years, and rather than follow a preconceived plan, it materialized as an improvisation upon which the client and the architect became closely related in ideas and views. Located in the midst of an urban environment, the garden connects to what was there before the city, offering points of entry to a past which has been repressed, thus connecting to the historic dimension.

The best sign for a prosperous architectural scene is the presence of young generations. Wang Hao's Wang House in Ningbo (2011) is a transformation of two farm houses in the village the architect grew up in. Made with local materials and built with local workers, the project is a symbol of the trend toward smaller-scale sustainable materials. The urban lifestyle and the memories of childhood merge into a new spatial experience.

Qian Fen Xi Rural Center for Social Aesthetics (2019) by Atelier Sounding Architecture (Liu Chang, Gao Qin, and Kong Dezhong) is again based on the transformation of existing buildings. It goes beyond the scale of a single house and includes a small part of a village. The connection between the new, open houses and the traditional constructions respect the existing pattern without merely conserving its substance. Terraces, passages, and steps connect the spaces. Atelier Sounding Architecture proposes a new typology by intertwining the spaces to follow the choreography of the tightly interwoven village neighborhoods, instead of being separate from each other like industrial spaces. The Multifunctional Hall and Waterfall Pavillon in Qinglongshan Park (2019) by Atelier XÜK (Liu Kenan and Zhang Xu) is located in a former limestone quarry, now transformed into a park. The muscular megastructure of the hall resonates with the dense infrastructure of the building and the rapid urbanization of the

Wang House by Wang Hao © Untitled Architects

boom period in China. The Waterfall Pavilion stands in contrast and recalls the traditions of domesticated nature with the garden. When I saw the images of these structures that highlight a huge, mostly artificial landscape, the scholar's rock came to my mind again.

Past and Present

As mentioned, one of the consequences of the discussion of the Anthropocene is that we cannot clearly distinguish between the natural and the artificial. Within the horizon of the Anthropocene, the traditional notion of nature as an endless and eternal resource does not make sense. Furthermore, the binary distinction between the city and the land collapses. For architectural theory, this is a challenge. As mentioned, architecture is deeply rooted in the thinking, the language and the ideologies of the colonization of the land. There is still no architectural theory based on the discussion of the Anthropocene.[1] However, many of the projects that I studied address this shift through the organization of space and the use of material. Can it be that the buildings know more than their authors, and us as observers? Do the porous stone surfaces, the tiles, and the terraces communicate with the rivers, the mountain ranges, the trees, and plants? Do they show us something that we cannot yet grasp in language?

According to Li Xiangning, professor and dean of the College of Architecture and Urban Planning, Tongji University, what is lacking are "critical discourses that not only recognize complicated cultural context and social reality in China," but which are also "comprehensible and meaningful to the Western audience."[2] How could such a critical discourse have developed? From Albert Lutz, a Swiss specialist on scholars' rocks, I learnt that "ancient Chinese belief saw everything animate and inanimate imbued with vital energy." This life force, called *qi*, as Lutz puts it, "flows not only through human beings and other living beings and plants (so long as they are healthy), but also through stones, mountains, water and air. Stones are regarded as the bones or the kernels of this flowing energy, and all these bones and kernels together form a 'skeleton' supporting the earth."[3] Can the scholar's rock then serve as an entry point for a more comprehensive story of recent and contemporary architecture in China?

The *Stones of Venice*, a three-volume book by the English art historian John Ruskin, written between 1851 and 1853, is a canonical work of European art history based on acute observation of the old churches and palaces of Venice. Could there be something similar in the

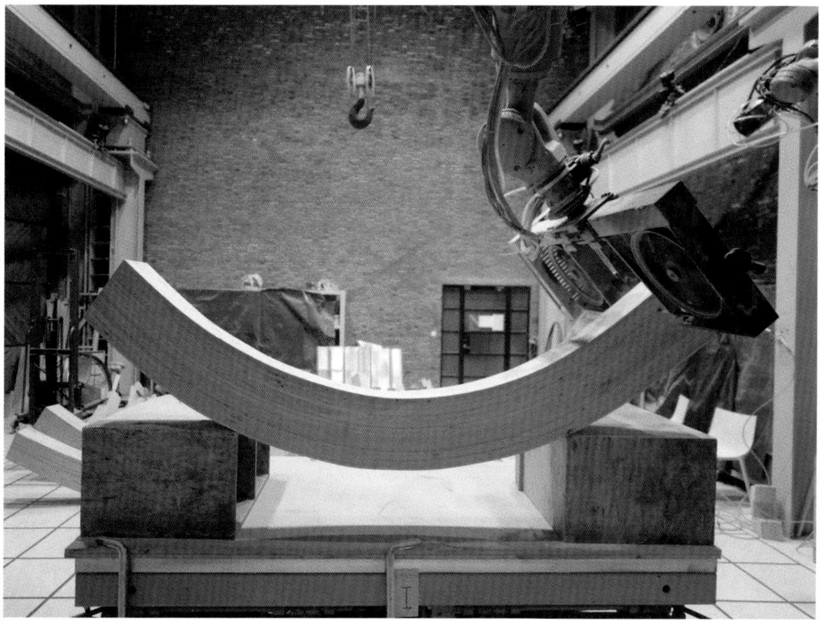

1. In Bamboo by Archi-Union Architects © Bian Lin
2. The wood beam of In Bamboo is being tested with robotic fabrication © Archi-Union Architects

China context? *A "Stones of China,"* perhaps? It could maybe be a critical study—not on the past, but on present-day architecture in China? The scholar's rock which mediates between reality and fiction, past and present, small and big, and human and non-human could function like a device to address this issue.

The present-day generation of architects in China are, more so than their colleagues in the West, certainly scholars. Most of them are well schooled and combine technological innovation with the knowledge of history. And most have witnessed the rapid growth and the rapid dismantling of the past more drastically than their peers in the West. Their work is about connecting. It mediates between the individual and the collective, between privacy and the public, between handicraft and high-tech, speed and slowness, and between Chinese culture and international culture. In many of the projects proposed in the 2020 Architecture China Awards, spaces are perforated and porous, and open for exchange and experiment. They help people to not only live more securely and comfortably, but also to reconnect with their environment, their past, present, and future.

1. This question is being researched by Helene Romakin in her doctoral thesis with the Department of Architecture at ETH Zürich.
2. Li Xiangning, "From 'experimental architecture' to 'critical pragmatism:' Practice of contemporary individual architects in China," in *Contemporary Architecture in China, Towards a Critical Pragmatism* (Victoria, Australia: Images Publishing, 2018), 7–13.
3. Philip Ursprung, ed., *Herzog & De Meuron: Natural History*, for Canadian Center for Architecture (Switzerland: Lars Müller, 2005), 109–117.

ARCHITECTURE CHINA AWARD IN PRACTICE

The Architecture China Award in Practice is the highest accolade presented in the Building with Nature – 2020 Architecture China Award. It honors an architect who has demonstrated "building with nature," or related concepts in his or her long-term architectural practice. It also requires that the architect has completed three or more high-quality works in the past ten years.

Liu Jiakun
Jiakun Architects

Laureate

Zhang Lei
AZL Architects

Shortlisted

Liu Yichun
Atelier Deshaus

Shortlisted

Liu Jiakun

Jiakun Architects
Founder and principal architect of Jiakun Architects

Jiakun Architects was founded by Liu Jiakun in 1999. Since its establishment, Jiakun Architects has continuously organized and participated in various international collaborations and exhibitions. As a multidisciplinary office, Jiakun Architects has worked with a range of international clients. The studio not only specializes in architectural design, but also in large-scale planning, urban, landscape, interior, and product design, as well as installation art. Focusing on social realities, Jiakun Architects always insists that architecture, which respects tradition, local context, and vernacular craftsmanship forms a symbiotic relationship with nature.

Furthermore, Liu Jiakun aims to solve contemporary architectural issues with a sense of realism for each project—an approach inspired by folk wisdom. His design vision integrates China's multiple cultures and traditions. Believing in the compatibility of tradition and modernity, Liu devotes himself to translating traditional Chinese cultural ethos into contemporary architectural language, which represents an elegant interweaving of individual and collective memories. His exploration of suitable technical approaches in architecture is purely the logical continuation of his professional work aiming to serve people in need. Many of these projects shine a light on the reciprocal relation between Chinese public life and urban cultural spaces.

Liu Jiakun's projects have been exhibited at many international exhibitions, such as the 15th Venice Biennale of Architecture and the 56th Venice Biennale of Art. Additionally, Liu designed the first pavilion for the Serpentine Pavilion Beijing in 2018. He has been longlisted for many domestic and international architectural awards, including the Honor Prize in the 7th ARCASIA, the 2003 Chinese Architecture & Art Prize, the Far East Award in Architecture, the Architectural Design Award from the Architectural Society of China, and the WAN Civic Buildings Award 2017: Best in Asia/PAC, among others. He has been invited to give lectures at Cité de l'Architecture et du Patrimoine, Massachusetts Institute of Technology, the Royal Academy of Arts, Palais de Chaillot in Paris, and many top universities in China.

Selected Works

2002 Luyeyuan Stone Sculpture Art Museum, Chengdu, China
2004 Department of Sculpture, Sichuan Fine Art Institute, Chongqing, China
2007 Jianchuan Museum of Cultural Revolution Clocks, Chengdu, China
2007 Hu Huishan Memorial Hall, Chengdu, China
2008 Rebirth Brick, China (in progress)
2010 Museum of Contemporary Arts (MoCA) Chengdu, Chengdu, China
2013 Shuijingfang Museum, Chengdu, China
2014 Novartis Shanghai Campus – Block C6, Shanghai, China
2015 West Village – Basis Yard, Chengdu, China
2016 Suzhou Imperial Kiln Ruins Park & Museum of Imperial Kiln Brick, Suzhou, China
2018 Serpentine Pavilion Beijing, Beijing, China
2020 Songyang Neighborhood Three-Temple Cultural Communication Center, Zhejiang, China
2020 Renovation of Tianbao Cave District of Erlang Town, Sichuan, China

1 | 2 / 3
1. Luyeyuan Stone Sculpture Art Museum © Jiakun Architecture
2. Hu Huishan Memorial Hall © Jiakun Architecture
3. With the Wind 2015 – It's Your Call © Jiakun Architecture

Interviewer: Fang Ziyu
Interviewee: Liu Jiakun (Liu)
Editor: Mo Wanli

What is your understanding of "building with nature?"

LIU: The relationship between nature and building is one of contradictions and balance. If you don't build, then there's nothing to talk about; if you have to build, then you have to work through the contradictions. Building poorly will harm nature; building well enables coexistence with nature; building even better will give cultural meaning to the environment. In that vein, building is still a matter of human effort that can achieve anything.

Cities arose from people's pursuit of combining efficient production and comfortable living. Today, cities serve as habitats for most humans; they are anthills that people have built for themselves. Broadly speaking, cities are also a part of nature. The architect's duty is to optimize these cities in terms of efficiency and energy-use. Otherwise, it defeats the purpose of the city and squanders the natural resources used toward that goal. Architects should also improve the habitats of such city dwellers through a more intimate scale, more hospitable spaces, more natural materials, and more ecological functions.

What are the main directions that your practice is currently exploring?

LIU: I want my work to be contemporary, universal, grounded, and rooted in my own cultural traditions, because my consciousness and subconsciousness as a modern-day Chinese person is something natural for me and what I'm most familiar with. This is actually dictated by my way of thinking. I've always worked in this direction and explored its propriety.

Jianchuan Museum of Cultural Revolution Clocks © Jiakun Architects

Can you talk about your low-tech strategy?

LIU: Our low-tech strategy emerged from a tactical approach to the specific construction realities in undeveloped areas of China. It helps guarantee that the final architecture will be faithful to its design and that it won't under-deliver. Because it carries on this approach, the low-tech strategy accepts, absorbs, and explores folk and handmade traditions, as well as less sophisticated things, thereby naturally adopting an unorthodox quality.

How do modern technology and traditional architecture influence and relate to each other?

LIU: Architectural cultural traditions are one element of the overall cultural traditions. We need a holistic understanding of the latter if we want to understand the former, or else we risk missing the forest for the trees. The architectural technology seen in the traditional architecture that have borne those traditions are largely the new technologies of its times. In other words, people in ancient times would certainly have used our technologies now, if only they had them at the time. I believe we should see the isomorphism of new and old technologies from different eras and use them harmoniously and naturally. Only this kind of traditional spirit is truly vivid and in step with the times, rather than becoming a physical symbol set in stone.

Songyang Neighborhood Three-Temple Cultural Communication Center © Arch-Exist

Renovation of Tianbao Cave District of Erlang Town © Arch-Exist

Within the context of globalization, what are the similarities that Chinese architects share with architects from the rest of the world in the way they approach, explore, and practice architecture?

LIU: By and large, Chinese architects today can work with the same universal technologies and within similar value systems adopted by non-Chinese architects, but they seemingly place a greater focus on discussions of "modernity vs tradition" and "Chinese vs foreign"—perhaps because in China, we are faced with a rupture and a clash of modernity and tradition. In comparison, Western architects tend not to have these discussions. Even if they're working in China, they work within their own traditions and only occasionally feature Chinese elements as localized embellishments. From this perspective, Chinese architects are still engaged to some degree in an identity struggle.

The only thing that you can really do well is doing what you know best, just like your native tongue compared to a foreign language. Chinese architects should emphasize their own local culture by developing and promoting their own excellence so that the world wants to embrace it, instead of using rejection and resistance to protect their own territory.

WEST VILLAGE

Location: 1 Basis North Rd, Qingyang District, Chengdu, Sichuan Province, China
Architect: Jiakun Architects
Principal architect: Liu Jiakun
Design team: Yang Lei, Jin Hongdong, Liu Su, Yang Ying, Cai Kefei, Hua Yi, Mao Weixi, Li Jing, Luo Ming, Wen Feng
Gross floor area: 135,552 square meters
Design and construction period: December 2009–September 2014
Photography: Arch-Exist

Courtyard of the West Village

West Village – Basis Yard is located at No. 1 Beisen North Road in Chengdu. With a length of 237 meters and a width of 178 meters, the project site takes up a full street block. The site is flat and surrounded by houses on all sides. Now serving as a center for communal sports, it used to host a golf driving range and a swimming pool, which has been retained and incorporated into the design. The development plan of the site allowed for a floor area ratio of 2.0, a land to building ratio of 40 percent, and a height limit of 24 meters.

The West Village project aims to create a spatial cluster for the organic local integration of sports and leisure, culture and art, and fashion and design. It combines collective memory, regional characteristics, and modern lifestyles to provide a suitable contemporary space for a diverse modern city and is a pacemaker that stimulates the vitality of this urban community.

Faced with the project's practical conditions, such as taking up an entire street block, being surrounded by tall buildings, and the height limit of the complex itself, the design resulted in an unusual centralized urban complex. The design maximizes an enclosed public space in the center and the use of the surrounding sidewalks for commercial purposes—a vitality that in turn profits the complex. Tall on the outside and low in the center, this 182-meter-long and 137-meter-wide circular building not only provides an urban green basin, which can accommodate a wide range of public activities, it also echoes the wider landscape of the local Sichuan Basin.

The building hosts two underground levels and five to six floors (depending on the building section) aboveground. The east, south, and west sides of the building continuously follow the boundaries of the project site, separating its internal spatial resources from the surrounding urban environment, forming a unique space within. The four gateway-like entrances on the ground floor and the elevated colonnade of the sloped runway on the north side connect the interior and the exterior, endowing West Village – Basis Yard with a simultaneously open and closed attitude.

The street-side façades of the complex host open corridors on each level, which allow each shop to have an independent storefront. The inward-facing side features a continuous balcony, which provides views of the central courtyard space. The wide balcony handrails are made of high-resistance bamboo, which provide a warm and natural feel, and can be used as seating to read or do work while overlooking the courtyard. The line of sight leads from outside in, creating the atmosphere of a stadium. The "bookshelf" framework design of the functional facilities enable diverse use and expression of communal creation. At the same time, the chaotic and complex behavior of individuals is framed by the spatial order of the huge courtyard. The design thus creates a rich and homogenized urban façade in which elements of daily life are performed on a monumental scale.

Aerial view of West Village

The construction of the framework tendons was based on functional practicality, economic structure, reasonable construction, and simple materials, while going beyond superficial design to create the aesthetic of an intrinsic shape. To achieve a higher floor height, create an open, flowing spatial atmosphere, and meet the flexible and diverse functional needs of the building, a new reinforced-concrete honeycombed-core girdless floor was applied. Handmade bamboo plywood commonly used in the area was adopted for the formwork, endowing the fair-faced concrete with a unique texture that enables the building to establish an abstract connection with its native surroundings. Widened structural cracks form artificial sceneries throughout the complex by revealing a single line of sky. The cracks simultaneously solve the problem of concealing and cooling the technical rooms. This design also showcases the concept of "physiological fractures" that was applied during the construction process. Using steel bars extracted from the concrete balustrade of the outer corridors as railings is a miniature expression of the same concept.

In the West Village complex, a large number of "rebirth bricks" are used for gables, parts of the solid walls, scenic pavement, and courtyard walls, thus serving a wide range of functions, such as enclosures, the outside of walls, ventilation, and greening. The reprocessed broken bricks expose their internal aggregate, making for a unique material appearance. In addition to "rebirth bricks," bricks with large holes are used for roof greening, ventilation in the machine room, and penetrable walls. Bricks with small holes are applied as foundation for the vertical gardens and bricks with multiple holes serve for fixing exhibits onto the gallery walls. Finally, gangue from coal mining, often used for basic filling purposes, serves as the material for the outer dry wall. The application of these materials not only saves costs and protects the environment, it also provides West Village – Basis Yard with a strong material authenticity. The extensive use of granite plaster and terrazzo continues a mature but nearly lost method of modern Chinese construction technology. The innovative application of locally used materials presents the building with both traditional and contemporary characteristics.

An existing building on the north side of the site was retained and transformed into a multifunctional art space. The circular complex is interrupted here only with the elevated running track filling the void. With a total length of 1.6 kilometers, the running track wraps around the courtyard, before climbing to the roof and completing the circle. It provides an exciting experience for runners and cyclists, while endowing the building with a dynamic energy.

Taking functional planning as the starting point, the landscape design incorporates bamboo spaces and teahouses as key concepts that represent Chengdu's local culture. The design aims to create a public place characterized by the city's lifestyle. As a native plant that represents

Running tracks

Aerial view of courtyard

1
2

1. Courtyard with bamboo
2. Street elevation

the local agriculture, bamboo is used extensively in the courtyard, expressing Chengdu's relaxed and comfortable temperament. In combination with the different types of bamboo, the courtyard is further separated into smaller areas marked by different floor types such as sand, cobblestone, and red sandstone. Small, medium, and large bamboo yards create a free, layered spatial experience, facilitating the much-loved local traditional pastime of relaxing under bamboo groves.

The landscape structure unfolds outwards from the center of the complex. A circular track surrounds the central multifunctional open-air space for sports, performances, and exhibitions, while a circular gallery makes up its periphery. The gallery's display walls consist of sandwich panels, which host the infrastructure for the small bamboo spaces dotted around the central area. The spaces covered by bamboo umbrellas are equipped with modern office facilities, thus forming bamboo teahouses, bamboo offices, and bamboo classrooms. Outside the inner ring, are five pockets of bamboo forest of different sizes that are planted with different bamboo species. A canal and a leisure zone follow the outer edge of the bamboo forests and serve as the connection and transition space between the building's ground floor and the inner courtyard.

Part of the running track extends to the top of the circular roof. The whole roof is paved with large-hole "rebirth bricks," which can be used for roof greening and urban gardening. It is also an abstract expression of traditional tiled roofs. The roof runway is additionally furnished with traditional Chinese garden elements such as pavilions, observation decks, corridors, covered bridges, and observation towers, which are reinterpreted with contemporary materials. Together, the circular roof and the inner courtyard form the huge green space that is West Village – Basis Yard.

As tall as the residential buildings around it, West Village – Basis Yard integrates into the surrounding neighborhood through its scale. The open entrances on all of its sides connect to the streets, creating a paradise for the local community. It's a place filled with vitality and a space with enormous growth potential.

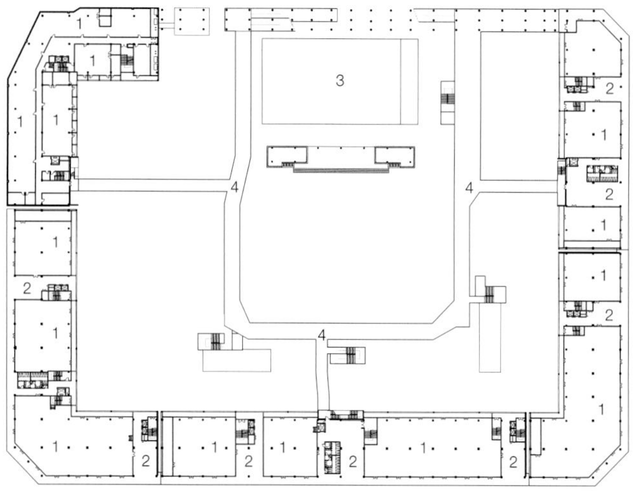

Second-floor plan

1. Commercial units and offices
2. Public space
3. Multifunction space
4. Track

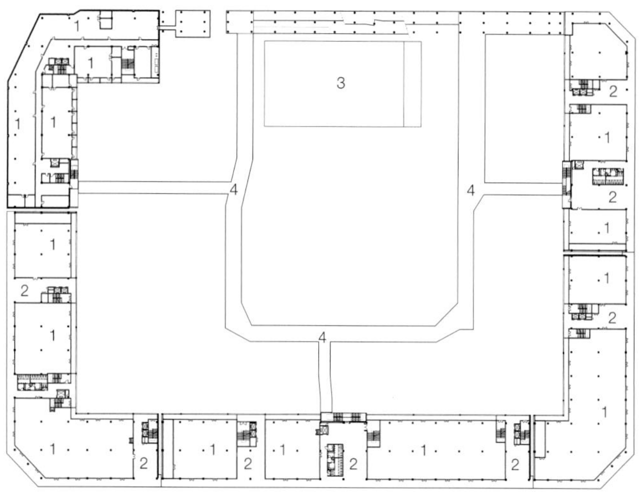

Third-floor plan

1. Commercial units and offices
2. Public space
3. Multifunction space
4. Track

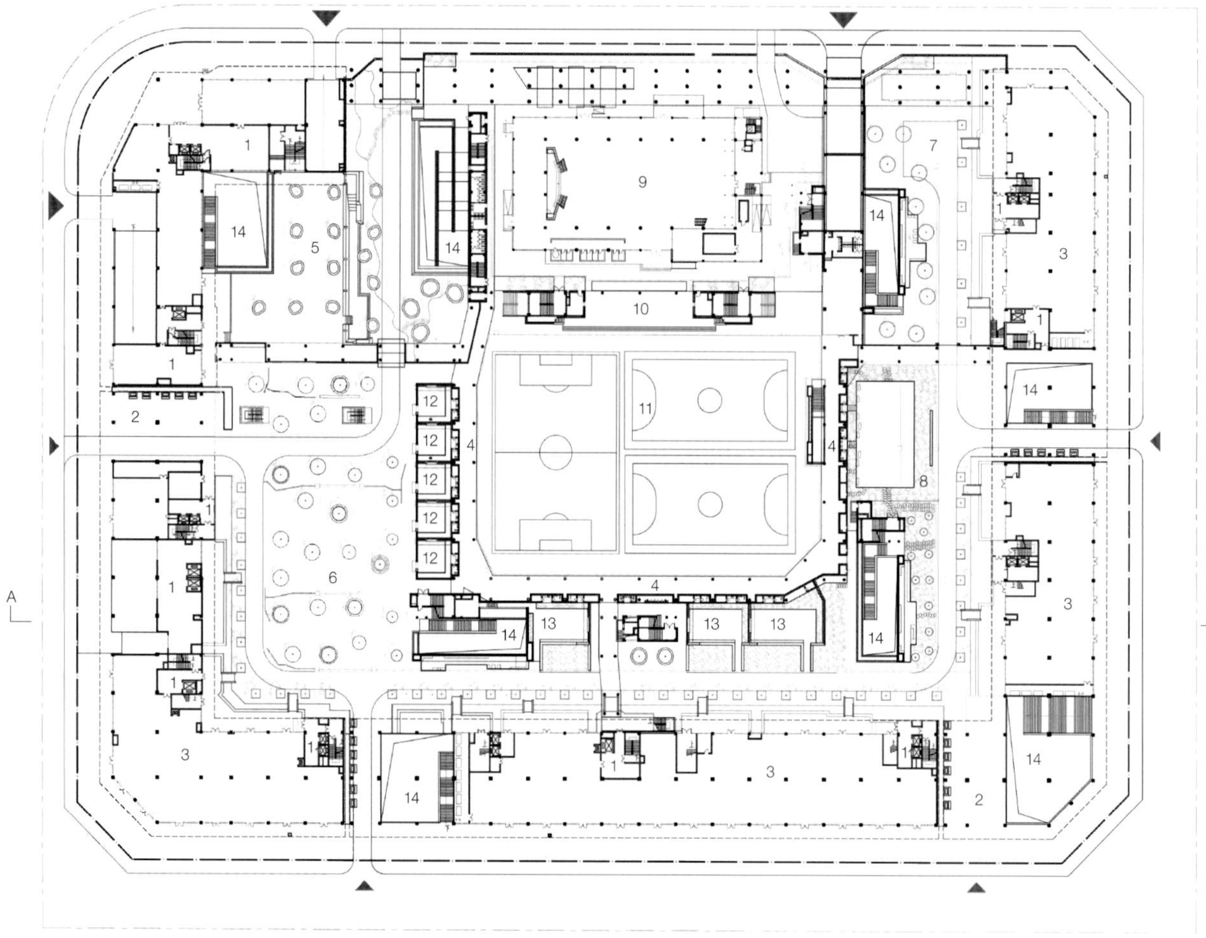

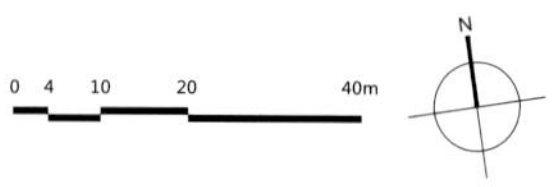

Ground-floor plan

1. Entrance hall
2. Stilt entrance
3. Commercial space
4. Gallery
5. Chungli bamboo yard
6. Affinis bamboo yard
7. Flavidorivens bamboo yard
8. Spotted bamboo yard
9. Multifunction space
10. Stage
11. Stadium
12. Small bamboo space
13. Large bamboo space
14. Sunk courtyard

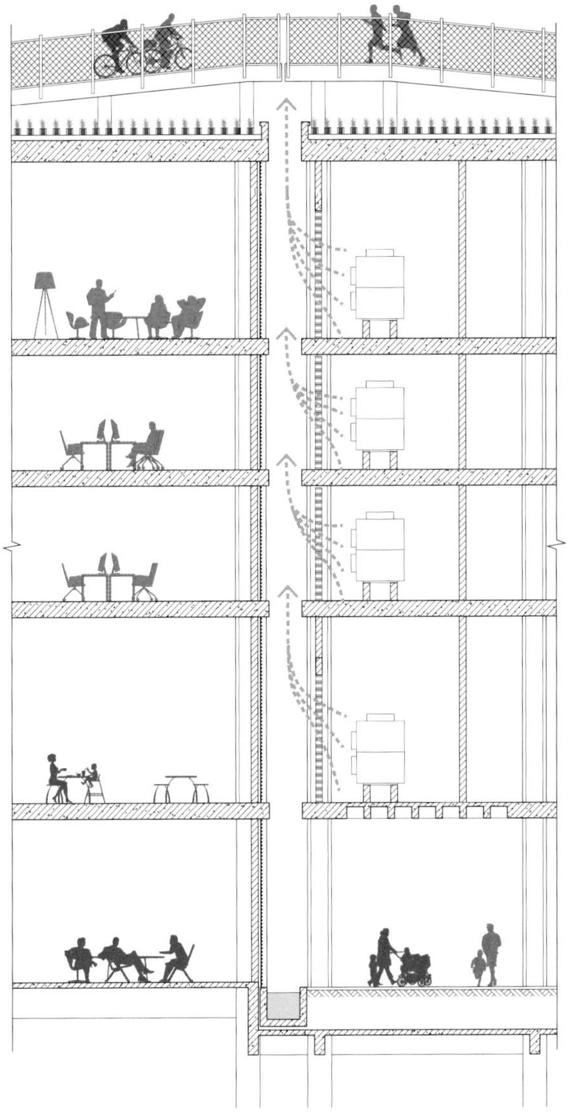

Detail section

Detail section

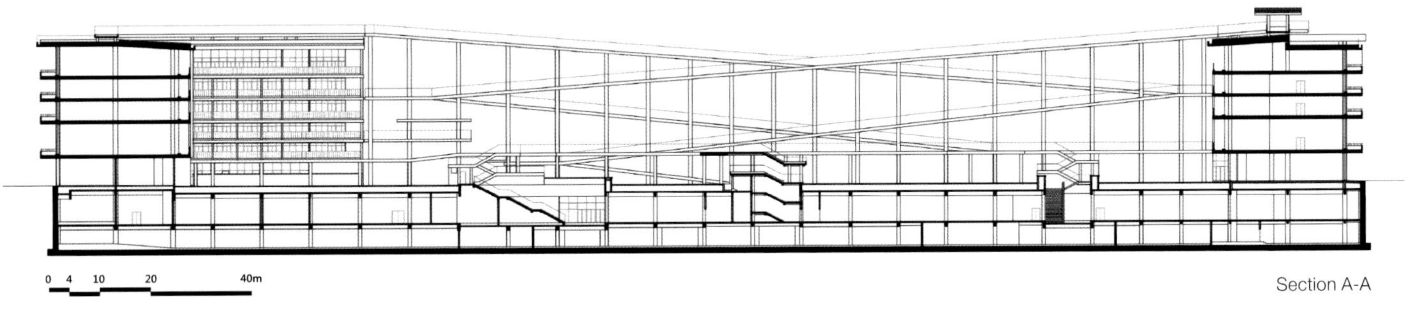

Section A-A

SHUIJINGFANG MUSEUM

Location: 1 Shuijingjie Street, Jinjiang District, Chengdu, Sichuan Province, China
Architect: Jiakun Architects
Principal architect: Liu Jiakun
Design team: Cai Kefei, Hua Yi, and Yang Dong
Site area: 12,148 square meters
Gross floor area: 8,670 square meters
Design and construction period: August 2008–April 2013
Photography: Arch-Exist

Site plan

Aerial view of Shuijingfang Museum

The site of the Shuijingfang Museum is located in the historical and cultural Shuijingfang neighborhood of Chengdu. It features ancient wells, gate towers, brewing workshops with timber frameworks built during the Republic of China period, and remains of wine cellars dating back to the 14th century (Yuan Dynasty).

The theme of the Shuijingfang Museum revolves around wine. Its main purpose is to display Shuijingfang's long history of winemaking and its precious unearthed cultural relics, and to protect and continue this traditional industrial heritage. The museum not only exhibits the traditional wine culture of the Chengdu Plain, but also enhances the cultural atmosphere of the entire Shuijingfang community.

Based on the architectural scale of the surrounding residential buildings, the complex uses small aggregated volumes to stitch together the fabric of this historic building complex. The design softens the boundaries between the single buildings through staggering, creating smooth transitions, and blending them with the texture of the protected area. Using the roofs of the surrounding residential houses as a model, the design consecutively deforms and distorts them. With a now continuous sloping roof, the complex forms a roof landscape consistent with the texture of the area's residential houses.

Remnants of the past can be found on-site and include a brewery from the Republic of China period and excavated ruins from the Ming and Qing Dynasties—among them a wine cellar that is still in use today. The cellar now represents an important part of the museum's presentation of industrial heritage. Together, these important cultural relics constitute the part of the museum used for the exhibition of ruins.

The entire design of the museum is based on the premise of protecting and respecting the cultural relics. The prudent and humble additions to the existing buildings are neither obtrusive nor simple imitations of the originals. They explore the coexistence between the old and the new on the basis of innovating inherited architectural characteristics. The new parts of the museum focus on creating a backdrop. The protective belt between the museum's new sections and the old workshops forms a set of alleyways similar to the ones in local residential areas. In an effort to create an appropriate backdrop for the cultural heritage within the site, the façade of the new buildings feature only a single material.

Inside the old timber-framed workshop, wine is still produced with traditional techniques, while contemporary brewing processes are used in the new concrete plant. The design of the new plant applies fair-faced concrete and a single-beam frame structure, echoing the traditional timber frame space of the original plant. The "lion's mouth" dormers

Interior corridor

Old wine workshop

of the new building are a refined version of the old factory's daylight openings. They create the same ventilation and lighting environment as the original, which is necessary for bacterial fermentation in the cellar. Together, the old and new buildings continue the historical development of winemaking, creating a living cultural heritage that integrates protection, display, production, and communication.

The movement of visitors through the Shuijingfang Museum is aligned with two different exhibition routes. The first is the sequence of the winemaking process, while the other is a chronology of the building's historic development. A boardwalk for visitors was built on stilts above the wine cellar and ruins area. The winemaking process below the boardwalk can proceed unhindered as the production line and visitor flow do not directly cross paths. Along the visitors route, one can get an overview of the entire wine production process from the fermentation stage in the cellar, to the storage of the base liquor, blending, and packaging.

The north side of the ruins area hosts a wine culture center with a patio as its architectural theme for spatial organization. Its form is adaptable, enabling its use for temporary exhibitions, academic conferences, and cultural exchanges. It also features a separate entrance to facilitate independent operation.

The design of the museum features short walls along the street and combines them with the existing Chinese scholar trees to maintain the original scale of the street and the atmosphere of the Shuijingfang neighborhood. The modest and peaceful entrance to the museum adopts the scale of residential buildings. The low wall encloses an entrance courtyard, which is paved with old bricks, creating a quiet corner in a noisy city.

Arranged alternately along the visitors route, the courtyards and exhibition halls create a relaxed atmosphere and a moderate spatial rhythm. The characteristic courtyards each represents a part of the rich culture of Sichuan province. Both the ancient well courtyard and the archway courtyard are equipped with independent patios, which not only emphasize the importance of cultural relics, but are also an important transition space between the indoors and outdoors, enriching the visitor experience.

The building uses contemporary materials that correspond to their traditional counterparts, for example "rebirth bricks" for gray bricks, heavy bamboo for wooden boards, and roof slates for small gray tiles. The museum continues and renews the traditional architectural temperament in order to create a building complex with modern techniques and historical charm.

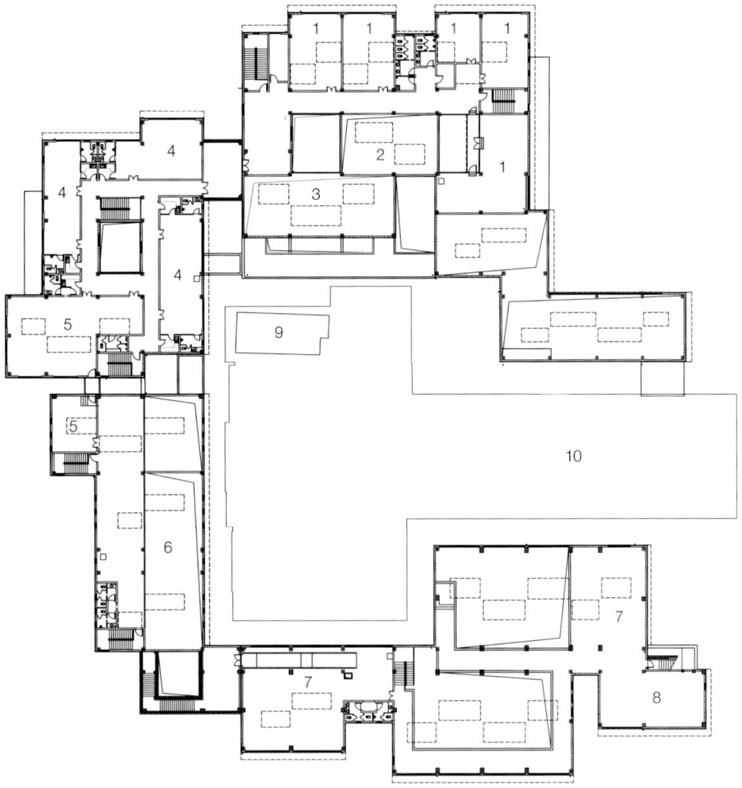

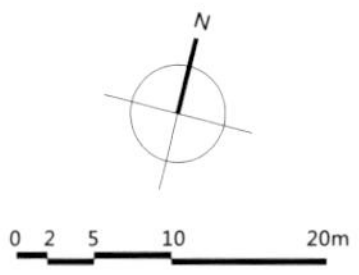

Second-floor plan

1. Laboratory
2. Lecture hall
3. Temporary exhibition
4. Office
5. Service
6. Research center
7. Exhibition hall
8. Multimedia room
9. Ruins
10. Old workshop

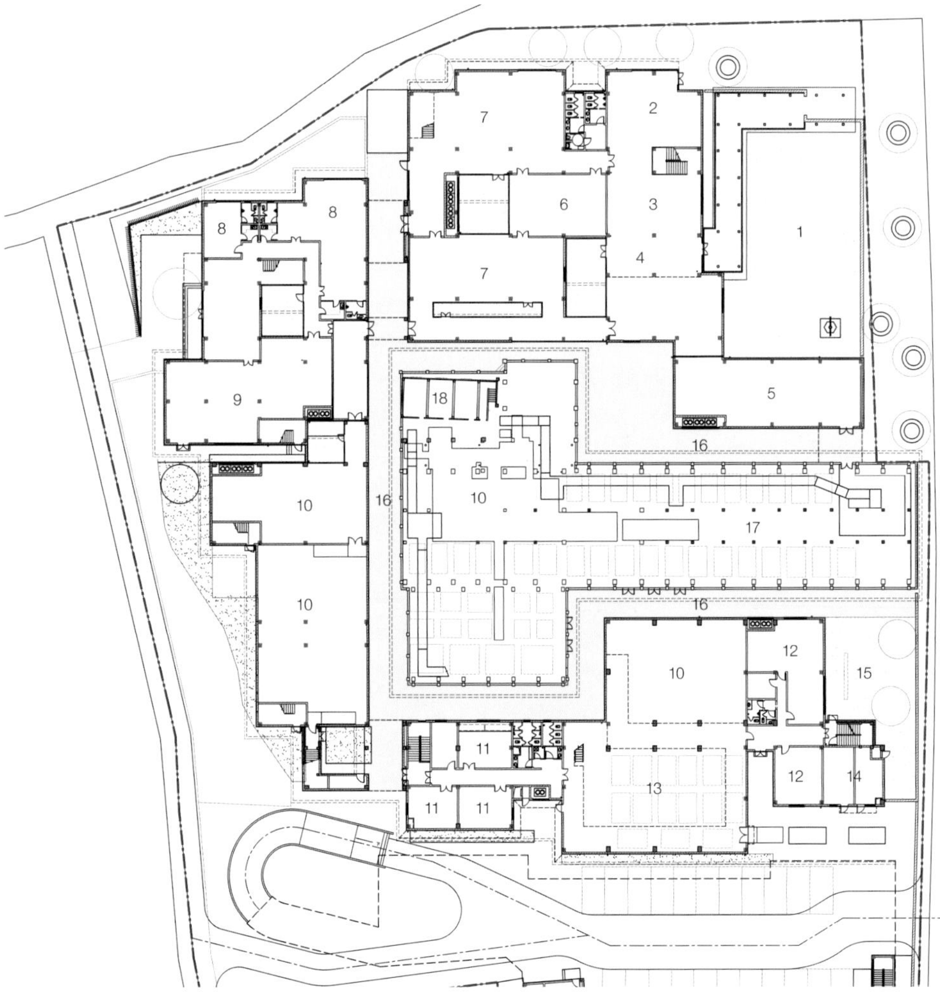

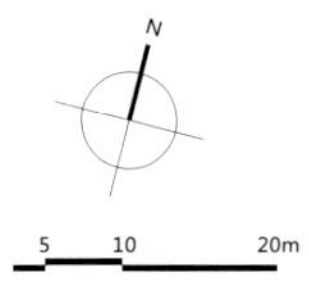

Ground-floor plan

1. Front yard
2. Shop
3. Lounge
4. Foyer
5. Lobby
6. Lecture hall
7. Temporary exhibition
8. Studio
9. Service
10. Relic exhibition hall
11. Storage
12. Office
13. New cellar
14. Cleaning supplies room
15. Courtyard
16. Buffer zone
17. Old workshop
18. Ruins

Atrium

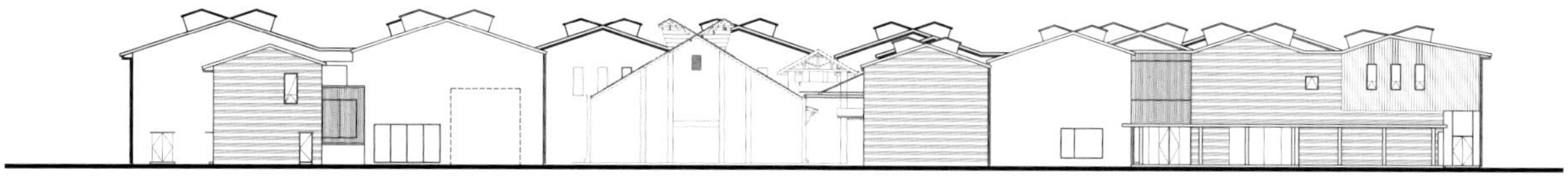

East elevation

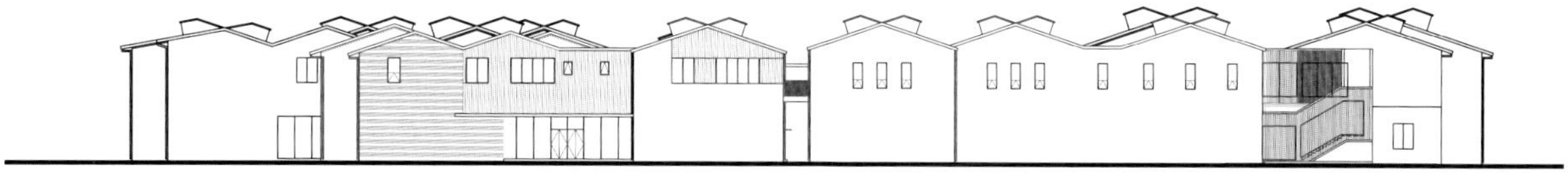

West elevation

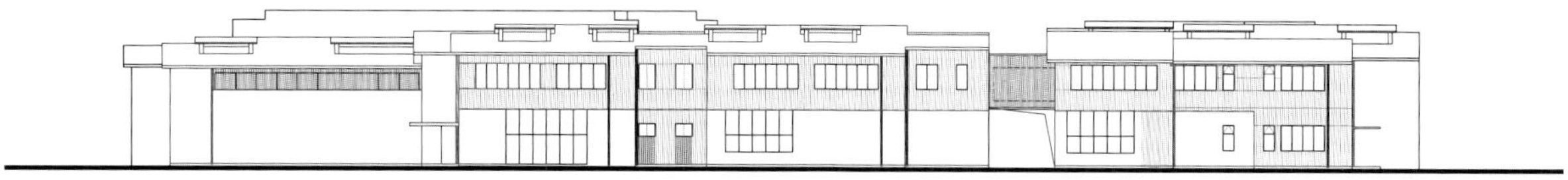

North elevation

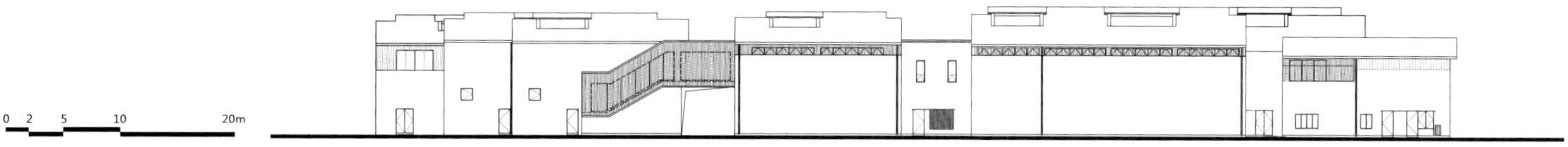

South elevation

SUZHOU MUSEUM OF IMPERIAL KILN BRICK

Location: Yuyaocun, Yuanhe St., Xiangcheng District, Suzhou, China
Architect: Jiakun Architects
Principal architect: Liu Jiakun
Design team: Tian Shen, Wang Xi, Liu Su, Yang Ying, Lin Yihsuan, Wang Kailing, Zhang Tong, Su Sihui, Xu Hao, Mao Weixi, Li Jing
Site area: 38,875 square meters
Gross floor area: 15,326 square meters
Design and construction period: January 2012–May 2016
Photography: Arch-Exist

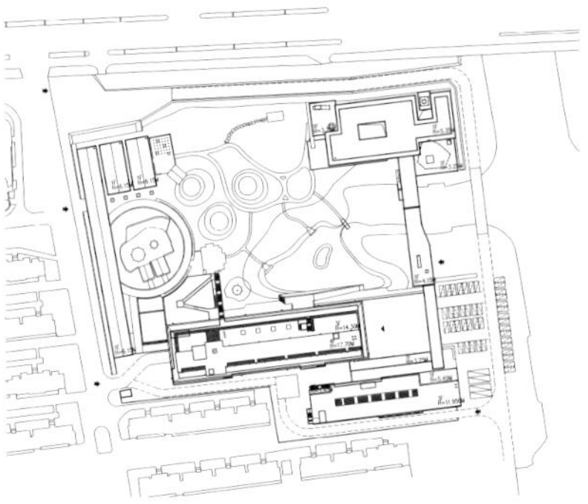

Site plan

North view of museum park

The Suzhou Imperial Kiln Ruins Park is located in the Xiangcheng District of Suzhou City. Its main functions include the protection and preservation of the imperial kiln ruins, the display of cultural relics such as the local "golden bricks," and related cultural research and exchange. Through the thoughtful organization of the buildings and the design of the landscape, the museum aims to protect the precious cultural relics, show the history of the imperial kilns and the "golden bricks," and present their historical and cultural connotation.

A layout in which the buildings surround a garden-like inward-facing space maximizes the size of the core protection area. To the north of the site, a tree-lined road near the bridge isolates the museum park from the city's hustle and bustle, creating a calm atmosphere, while the large volumes of the buildings hides the residential compound to the south. Internally, the distribution of the production facilities and the group of kilns guide the visitor's line of sight. The design of the visitors route winds through the site, leading to secluded spaces, continually changing the view.

Bridge

The main museum building is a comprehensive combination of a brick kiln and a palace. Its volume is magnificent, while its eaves are flat. It uses modern methods to interpret traditional meaning. It is not a brick kiln nor a palace, but a contemporary public building that incorporates the feelings of both types of building, presenting the spiritual connotation of an imperial kiln.

The museum complex uses a variety of brick materials widely used in contemporary construction. Layer after layer, it showcases the imperial "golden bricks." It is not only a museum for these bricks, but also a chronicle of brick making from antiquity through modern times.

The landscape design emphasizes the sense of heritage. Its natural wildness serves as a metaphor for history and protects the original appearance of the imperial kiln ruins. Within the park, a sense of community is created through the kilns in various states of preservation, such as complete, semi-preserved, and residual. They recreate a lively brick production scenery from the past, while the structure of the kilns and the production process of the bricks can be explored from various perspectives, so as to expand the knowledge base of the museum itself.

Foyer

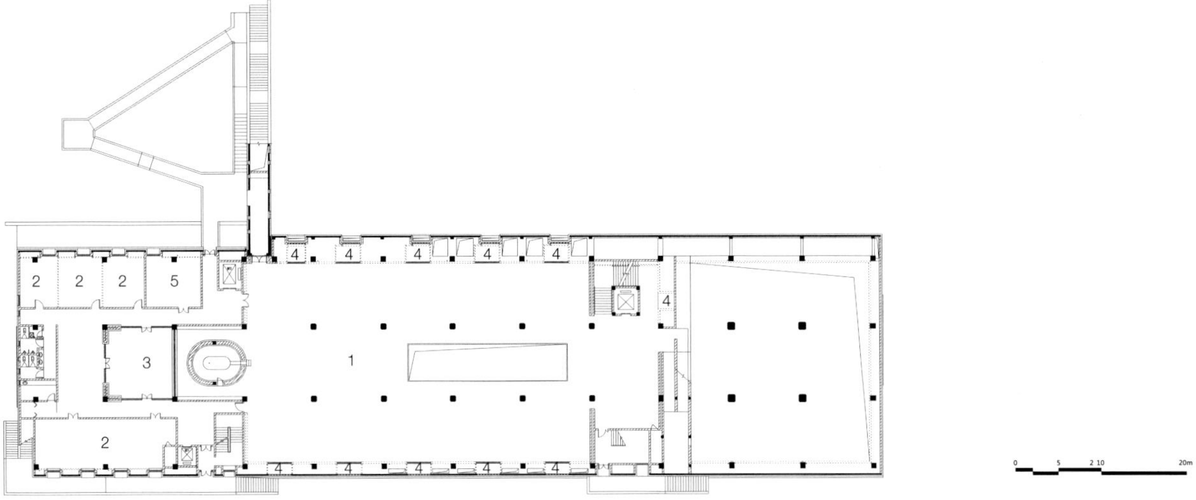

Second-floor plan

1. Exhibition hall
2. Office
3. Courtyard
4. Niche
5. Equipment

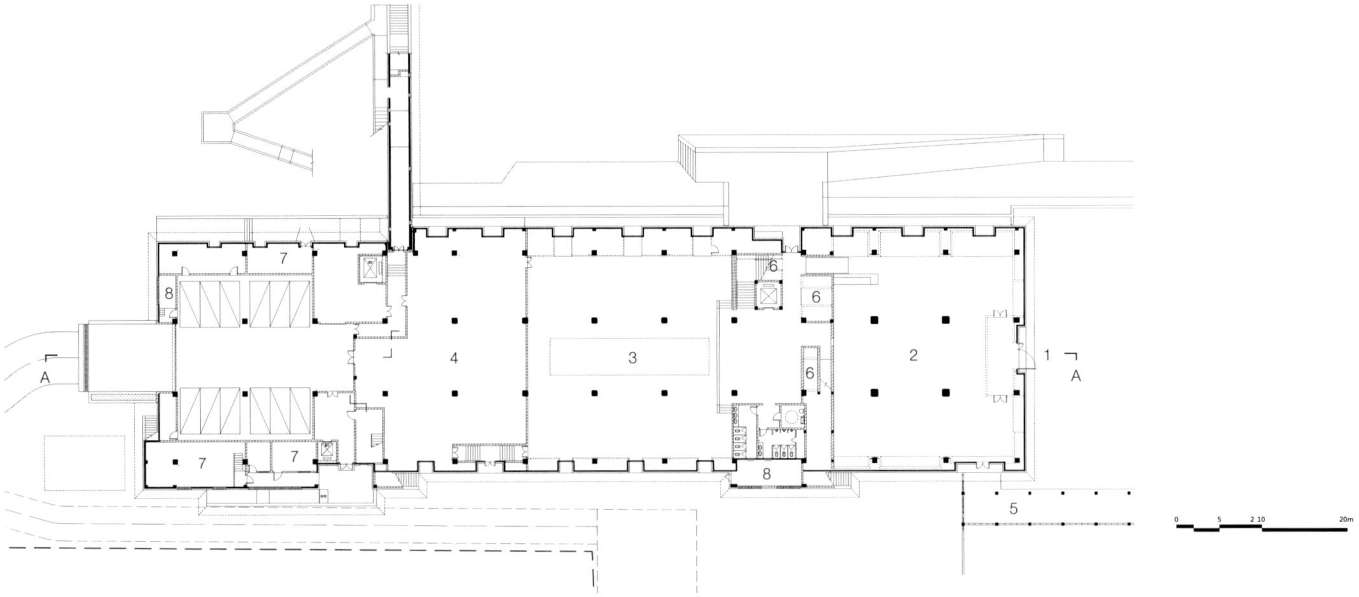

Ground-floor plan

1. Barrier-free main entrance
2. Preface hall
3. Exhibition hall
4. Library of collections
5. Bridge
6. Niche
7. Equipment
8. Air conditioner

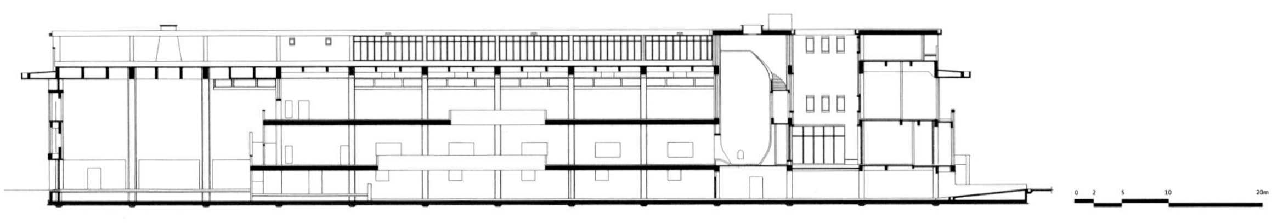

Section A-A

Spiral staircase

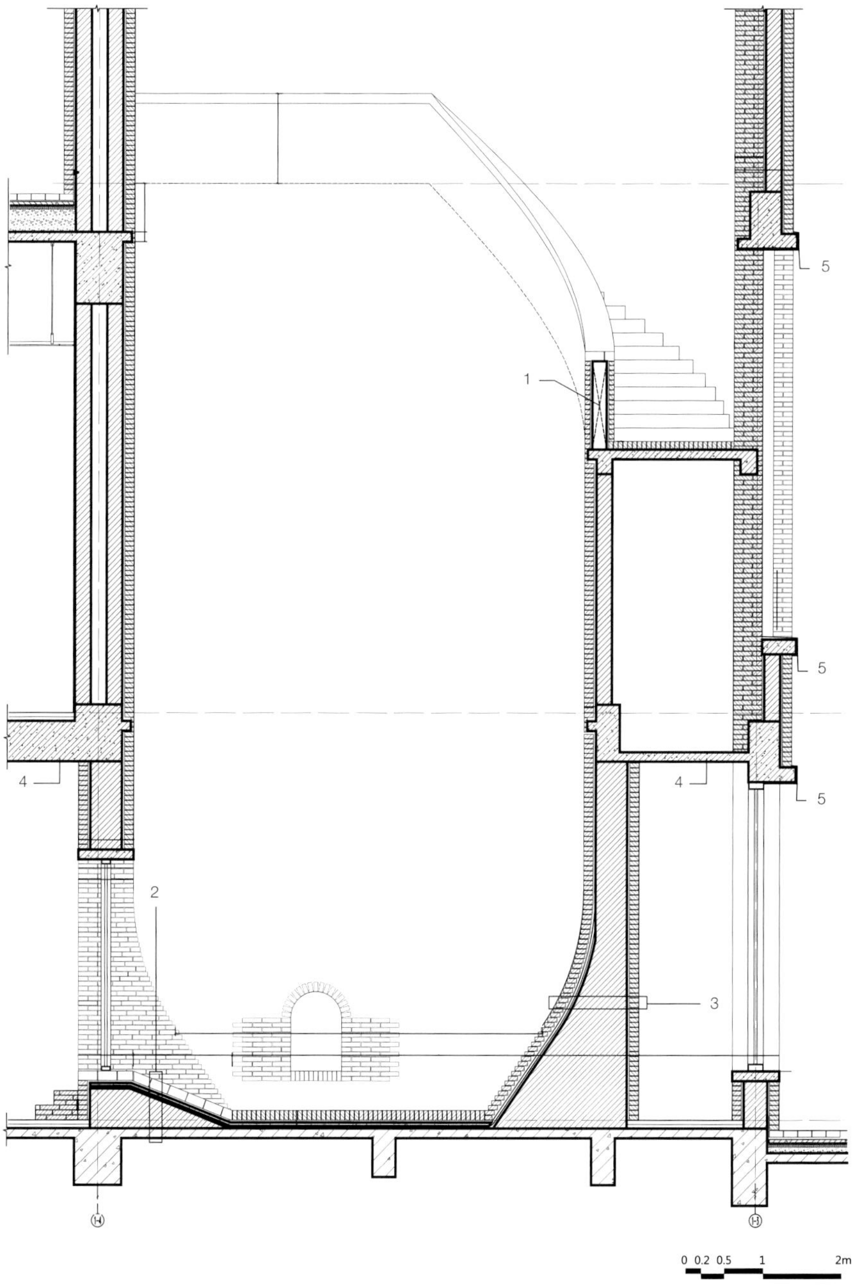

Brick kiln detail

1. Structural column
2. Solid clay brick (240x115x57 mm)
   30 mm cement mortar
   40 mm fine aggregate concrete
   10 mm gray mortar separation layer
   3 mm sbs bituminous waterproof sheet
   20 mm cement mortar
   reinforced-concrete
3. Solid clay brick (240x115x57 mm)
   30 mm cement mortar
   10 mm gray mortar separation layer
   3 mm sbs bituminous waterproof sheet
   20 mm cement mortar
   Interior wall of porous brick
   Solid clay brick (240x115x57 mm)
4. Bamboo plywood with fair-faced concrete
5. Drip

Zhang Lei

AZL Architects
Founder and principal architect of AZL Architects
Professor, School of Architecture & Urban Planning, Nanjing University

After teaching design, studying abroad, and researching architecture through the 1990s, Professor Zhang Lei founded an architecture studio at Nanjing University in 2000, gradually shifting his focus to architectural practice. After nearly a decade of continuous development, his studio has not only grown into a pioneering design firm with international influence, but it has also become an influential representative of contemporary Chinese architecture. AZL Architects was formally established in 2009 with offices in Nanjing and Hangzhou. The goal of Zhang Lei's unremitting efforts include to actively respond to the needs of sustainable human development; contribute a forward-thinking analysis of resources, cultures, cities, residences, commerce, and markets; show the charm of design with wisdom and responsibility; and maximize environmental, social, cultural, and economic benefits.

AZL Architects was recognized as one of ten architecture offices for the 2008 Design Vanguard by *Architectural Record.* In 2012, Zhang Lei was named a candidate for the 4th Swiss Architectural Awards. Zhang Lei has participated in major international exhibitions on contemporary Chinese architecture in the Netherlands, France, Germany, Italy, and the United States. His works are widely published in international magazines such as *GA Document, Domus, Lotus, Architectural Record, Architectural Design,* and *Architectural Review,* to name a few.

Selected Works

2003 Model Animal Genetic Research Center of Nanjing University, Nanjing, China
2007 Brick House, Nanjing, China
2007 Concrete Slit House, Nanjing, China
2011 Zhengdong New District Urban Planning Exhibition Hall, Nanjing, China
2011 Nanjing CIPEA No. 4 House, Nanjing, China
2014 Nanjing Wangjing Garden Chapel, Nanjing, China
2015 Longhu Financial Center C4-06, C4-15 Mansion, Nanjing, China
2016 Shitang Internet Conference Center, Shitang, China
2017 LEI House, Tonglu, China
2018 Song House, Shanghai, China
2019 Future Stitch Smart Factory, Haining, China
2019 Bingding Wood Kiln, Jingde Town, China
2019 Museum of Nanjing University, Nanjing, China
2019 Museum of Chinese Drama of a Hundred Plays, Nanjing, China
2020 Tengchong Multifunctional Cultural Center, Tengchong, China
2020 Shijiazhuang CBD Exhibition Hall, Shijiazhuang, China
2020 Nanjing Ruralation Tangshan Museum Resort, Nanjing, China

Bingding Wood Kiln © Yao Li

Interviewer: Fang Ziyu
Interviewee: Zhang Lei (Zhang)
Editor: Mo Wanli

What is your understanding of "building with nature?"

ZHANG: "Building with nature" is a meaningful proposition because it contains criticisms within itself. "Nature" and "building" are inherently contradictory, as buildings of any kind destroy nature. The only thing linking those together is time; its restorative function can reduce the contradiction between the two and the damage wrought by "building." My understanding of "building with nature" has to do with time: the light that changes with time, the mark of time left on materials and textures, the unity of content and form in the face of time, and the continuous growth of nature over time. The essence of "building with nature" is the constant perception of new needs on time.

All matter that existed before today has some attribute of nature; they're all a part of nature. Aside from its restorative function, time can also connect things, weaving together past and future to create context. I believe in the idea of building with nature, which is similar, in essence, to "new organic architecture" and time.

Concrete Slit House © Iwan Baan

Shitang Internet Conference Center © Hou Bowen

What are the main directions that your practice is currently exploring?

ZHANG: The experiences and explorations of my practice in recent years have been about "new organic architecture," which looks at the sameness that comes from form and public spaces, the relationship between people, architecture, and the external world, and the coexistence of architecture and nature. Within that, the form is the place, the ritual is the context, and the paradigm is nature. I started exploring "form as the site" in 2011 with the Zhengdong District Urban Planning Exhibition Hall, which features a continuous walkway extending from the street intersection to the roof. That design offered a starting point for thinking about the relation between form and place. Later, two high-rise financial offices on Longhu Financial Island in Zhengdong New District also attempted something similar with their external and internal space. Collected perceptions of time, gathered through my practice in rural areas, led to those two latter experiences. They are different in two ways: one points at the relationship between architecture and the outside world, while the other explores the coexistence of architecture and nature.

How do you approach "new organic architecture" in conjunction with "building with nature?"

ZHANG: The three main elements of "new organic architecture" offer three points of reference. "Form as site" means creating more common spaces within a dense, urban environment and connecting the focus on architectural form to the construction of shared public places. Thinking about the relationship between people, architecture, and the outside world is a way of experiencing a better world within an architectural design framework; to put it simply: man becomes one with nature. This has nothing to do with architectural scale or urban density.

The most effective way for us to perceive time is to leave more room for nature to grow and coexist with architecture. I'm often moved by what I see at the construction sites: once all the thick mud has been removed, grass can sprout from these soilless cracks. We need to leave space for nature and allow it to grow with our architecture.

Song House © Yao Li

Nanjing CIPEA No. 4 House © Yao Li

How do you understand the relationship between modern technology and traditional construction?

ZHANG: Not that long ago, constructing was a survival skill and a tool for human interaction. Architecture remains one of the few constructs for which the completion relies entirely on manual labor and an industry where manual manufacturing can rival advanced construction technology. Traditional architecture and modern technology are two lines of parallel development that often intersect. One such project where those two facets came together is Ruralation Xiaoxiongbao in Tonglu, Zhejiang. The structure itself was hand-built by She-minority stonemasons, while the pavilion was 3D-printed and shipped over for on-site installation.

LEI HOUSE

Location: Tonglu City, Zhejiang Province, China
Architect: AZL Architects
Principal architect: Zhang Lei
Design team: Ma Haiyi, Zhong Huaying, Liu Ying, Yuan Ziyan
Gross floor area: 296 square meters
Design period: 2016–2017
Completion: October 2017
Photography: Yao Li, Hou Bowen

Site plan

LEI House and its context

Despite the enormous amount of urban development in China's cities over the last three decades, the country's villages rooted in traditional agriculture still maintain the overall rural characteristics of "architecture with no architects." They represent a kind of primal order influenced by the traditional social background that is now clashing with urban civilization. The LEI House is one such instance worth highlighting. It is located in Shanyinwu Village of Tonglu County in the eastern city of Hangzhou, not far from the village center. Most of the houses in the village have been rebuilt within the last ten years and show signs of the typical "new rural" style. From an architectural perspective, features of the local architectural tradition are nearly invisible.

The site of the project is that of an ordinary village house. It stands on a platform that is about 200 square meters in size, backed by the hillside, and which faces a valley and a water reservoir. The owner plans to use the house as a residence, while also providing accommodation for travelers. Ms. Lei, the homeowner and founder of the successful local bed and breakfast brand Ruralation, is an influential next-generation rural-returnee. She hopes to demonstrate the value of projects such as this one as a model for rural economic development and environmental improvement. This is also an opportunity for the development of the village that the inhabitants have longed for.

The layout of the site follows the arrangement of basic village farmhouses. It faces the valley and main road on the south side, while forming an open courtyard backed by the hills. The square-shaped three-story building aligns with the neighboring houses on both sides. Except for the easily visible vegetables and flowers planted in the yard and on the roof, this gray stone object is difficult to notice compared to its white-and-red decorated neighbors.

LEI House features a brick and concrete structure that is commonly used by local artisans. The three stories, the simple vertical volume, and few window openings, together with the exceptionally compact interior space, are reminiscent of traditional local rammed-earth houses. Thanks to free stone bits from a local stone processing factory and skilled craftsmen in the area, the construction of this castle-like house, which provides the homeowner with a sense of security and belonging, had

LEI House front view

very limited additional costs. The efficient use of the interior space and the flexible arrangement of the stairwell inside the house smoothly connects the functional spaces on each floor. Natural light enters from the top and side windows, reaching each corner of the house to provide an interesting spatial experience.

Arriving on-site at the mere cost of transportation, the blue-gray stone slates are the scraps of a nearby stone processing factory; the stone is usually used to decorate urban buildings, roads, and public squares. The dry masonry work is not only a continuation of the local She-minority tradition of wall and dam construction, but also an introspection on new brick veneers for farm houses. The successful use of the stone bits in LEI House led to the rise in price for such scrap pieces from the neighboring stone factory. Seems, the factory that had previously only provided materials for urban construction discovered unexpected opportunities from an untapped local demand.

The Bauhaus-style bamboo chandelier is from a skilled bamboo craftsman in the village and is the result of arduous attempts (guided by Ms. Lei's directions) to get right. The rooftop garden of LEI House utilizes a thick soil in which vegetables thrive without fertilization or pesticides, while most of the neighboring farmers depend heavily on those chemical additives.

Confronted with new technologies, especially the sudden appearance of superior industrial products, native construction techniques practiced by individuals easily lose popularity. The heavy use of concrete blocks in the surrounding wall and in the landscape design of LEI House aims to re-establish the connection between technology and craftsmanship. The hollow concrete blocks are usually a cheap construction material in rural areas, but after being reconfigured by the architects and the craftsmen, they perform just as well as masonry in terms of spatial composition and expressiveness.

3D-printed pavilion

1
2 | 3

1. Solid and translucent materials
2. View toward the entrance
3. Entrance lobby

A masonry logic is also applied in the 3D-printed tea pavilion in the courtyard. The 3D-printed polylactic acid (PLA) units replace the usual building blocks and aim to further emphasize the transparency of the hollow bricks. The translucent space and material are achieved through the combination of precise digital control and flexible, manual adjustment of scale and single components. No matter what technological invention, its efficiency will always be judged on two levels: First, is the fact that its own physical properties form the basis. Yet, even more important, is the setting of its parameters, as well as the possibility of optimization. This could be a way of eliminating the contradiction between technology and craftsmanship.

A limited budget, the lack of professional management teams and the continuous outflow of skilled local craftsmen are common problems faced by rural construction. Based on 3D printing technologies, an industrialized prefabrication system, off-site processing, and supply chain logistics, the on-site assembly minimizes the damage caused by construction to the local environment. In the front yard of LEI House, the 3-by-3-by-3-meter cubic tea pavilion was constructed out of 400 square-shaped units. They were produced within one month through the cooperation of three suppliers in Beijing and Nanjing, with inexperienced workers being able to complete the final assembly within three days. Efficiency-oriented and supported by modern technology, the architects were able to successfully explore the direction of rural construction under its constrained conditions.

The time and material consumption of 3D printing directly affected the project's timeline and construction costs. In line with the practical conditions of rural construction, often small and lacking professional equipment, losing "weight" became the core pursuit of the design of the pavilion. With the adjustable density of 3D-printed objects, the corresponding parameters were set according to the load-bearing requirements of each building unit and to create a translucent effect. The transparency and texture of the pavilion contrast sharply with the heavy volume of the dense castle-like stone walls of the main building. In the rural setting, their extremely simple forms enhance each other, creating a pure, pristine, yet reserved and mysterious atmosphere of a village of the future.

On humanity's long way back to nature, rural settlements provide a naturally advantageous spiritual shelter. With their anti-commercial tradition, low-tech approaches, and the desire to reshape their communities, the craftsmanship in rural architecture and technologized villages can be an effective path to remodeling sustainable human spaces.

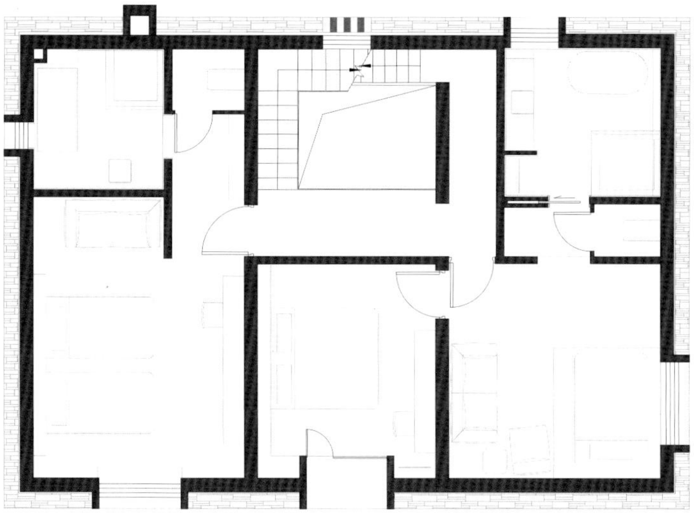

Third-floor plan

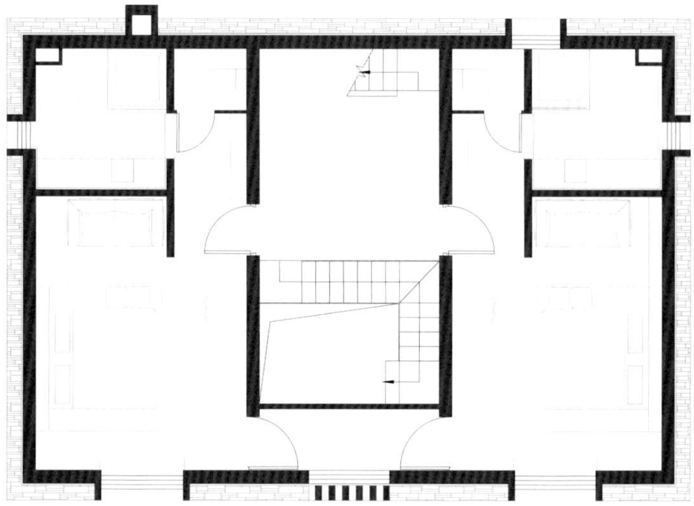

Second-floor plan

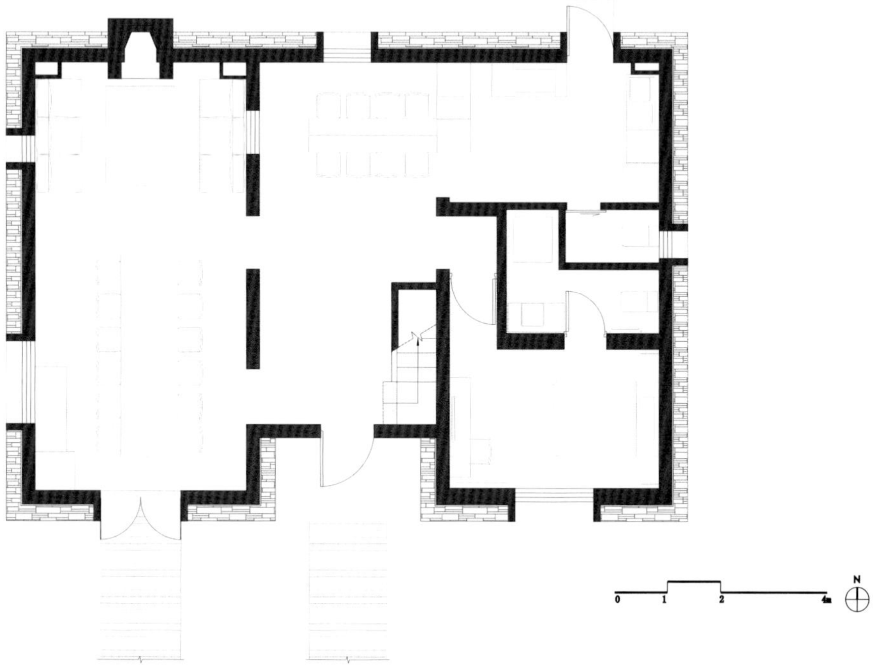

Ground-floor plan

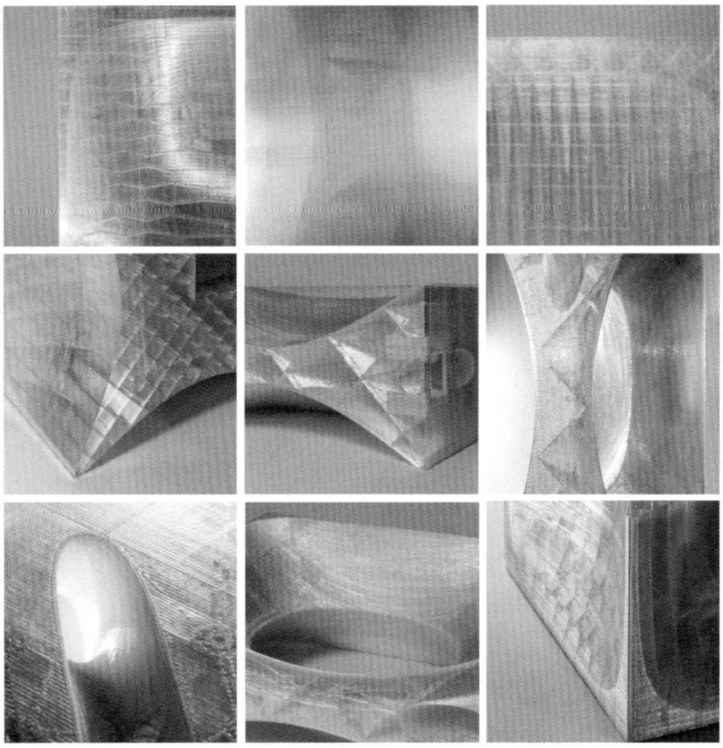

Model

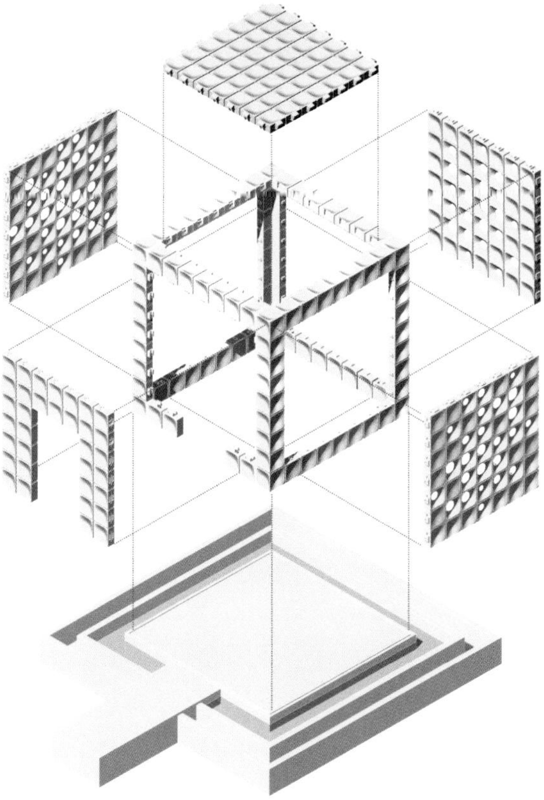

Axonometric diagram of the 3D-printed pavilion

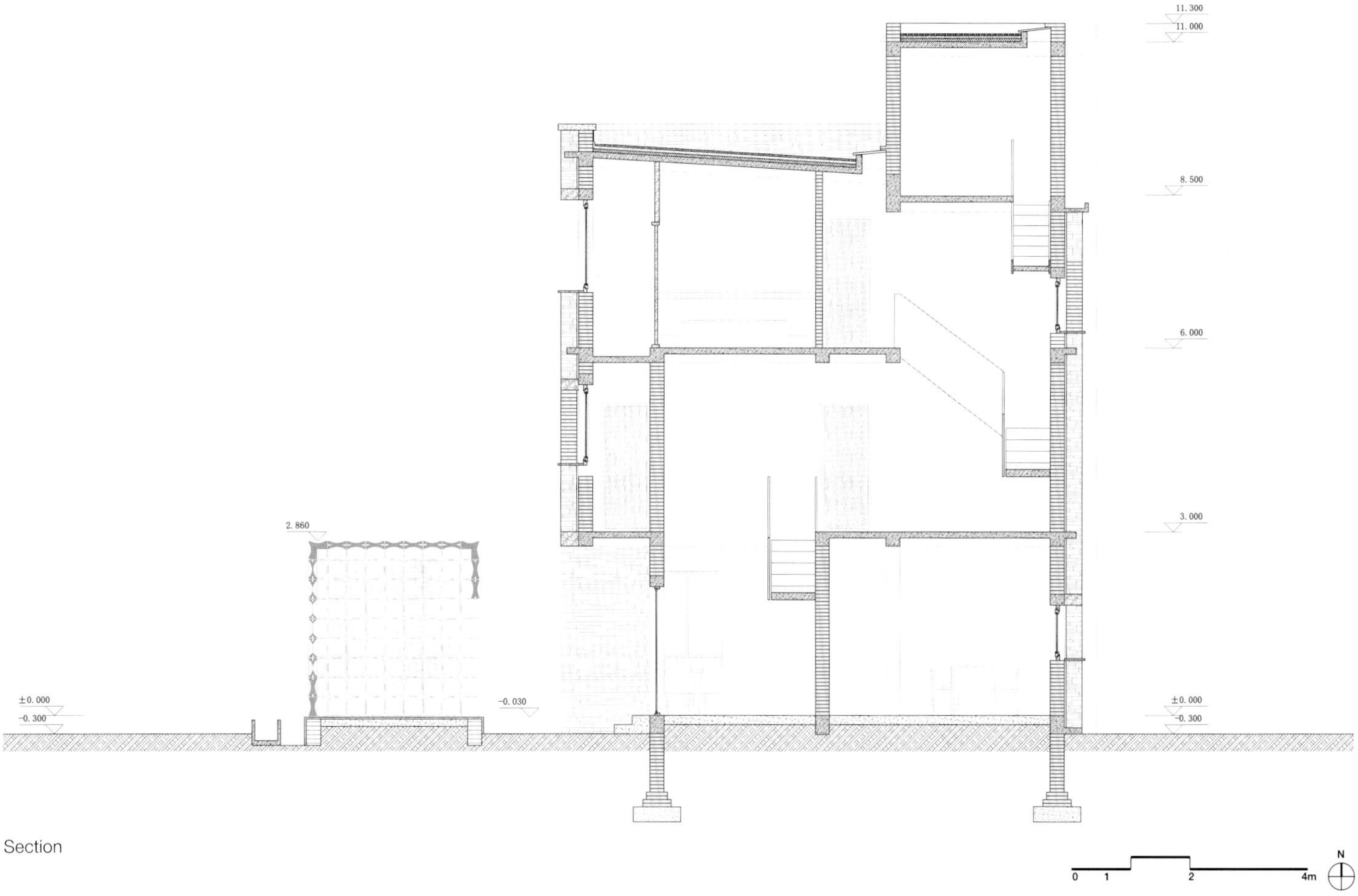

Section

NANJING WANJING GARDEN CHAPEL

Location: Nanjing, Jiangsu Province, China
Architect: AZL Architects
Principal architect: Zhang Lei
Design team: Wang Ying, Jin Xin, Cao Yongshan, Hang Xiaomeng, Huang Longhui
Collaborator: Institute of Architecture Design and Planing Co., Ltd. of Nanjing University
Project area: 200 square meters
Completion: 2014
Photography: Yao Li

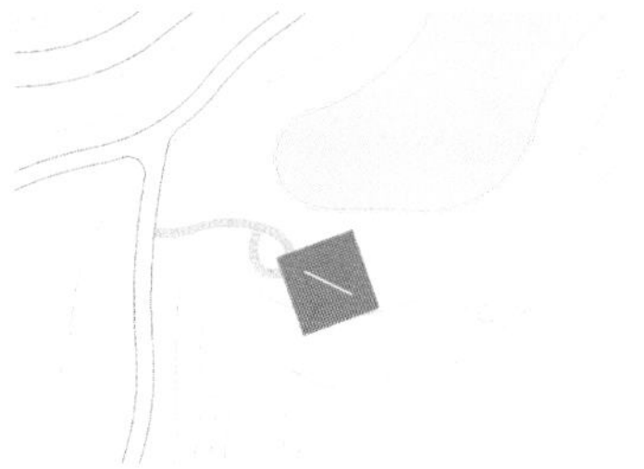
Site plan

This 200-square-meter chapel is located in Wanjing Garden along Nanjing's Riverfront. Hosted by priests from Nanjing Union Theological Seminary, it supports religious activities that include worship and wedding services. This wood-and-steel-structured chapel has a gentle exterior shape, as well has a strong interior space infused with mysterious religious power. Its plain material doesn't fail in expressing the delicate construction logic.

The earliest and fundamental church space had two interrelated tendencies: center and depth. Both the centrality from the Pantheon and the deep axis of a typical Basilica were inherited during the time of early christian architecture. The central and axial symmetry of the church space became less prominent during the modernism period, which was closely related to the Prostestants' rejection of Catholic hierarchy. In the design of Wanjing Garden Chapel, the architect didn't purposefully reject the centrality and depth of classical square-shaped; in plan, it has an octagonal central hall surrounded by square-shaped corridors; in section, the use of roof profile and the long slit of skylight amplify the depth of space and emphasize the high point over the sacred space where all axis meet.

The wooden corridor forms a unique double-shell around the central hall space. The inner shell is more closed, leaving natural light to penetrate only through openings in the roof and walls. The outer shell, composed of delicate SPF strips, serves as a filter of the view outside, implying the start of a religious spatial experience. The double-shell system creates a uniquely interesting oriental architectural space that's different from the closedness of a traditional stone chapel, or the openness of modern architecture. The small chapel has a perfectly square-shaped plan. Even with the 45-degree turning connecting inner space to exterior structure, the square remains highly integrated, symmetrical and center-oriented. A hidden diagonal axis in the plan also extends to the roof structure, realizing a complete integrity of space, material and power.

Light is an important component in the religious expressions of church space. In this particular design, light falls through the strip skylight right above the axis of the altar into the center of the hall, and also penetrates from behind the holy cross on the altar wall. The presentation of this 300-millimeter-wide light strip is the most powerful defining element of the interior space. Natural light also gently filters through the wood strips into the openings on the wall.

Using wood strips for construction is a wise choice when working within a tight project schedule and limited budget. Roof structure composed of less costly material open the way for natural light and add expressiveness to the entire space. All interior surfaces are painted white, emphasizing the leading role of light and space. The exterior wood strips and asphalt shingles are left in their natural color, emphasizing the importance of nature. The SPF strips surrounding the church are so delicate that their length-to-radius ratio could be 1:120, largely exceeding the normal load bearing. With lengths as long as 12 meters and a section area only 39-by-39 millimeters, the strips are connected to the roof and ground by metal parts at both ends, keeping them in their ideal stretching status. Adjacent wood strips are also connected with U-shape metal parts to insure stability. These together achieve a metal-wood structure that's extremely simple in material selection and installation.

As a religious institution with very simple functions, this small chapel has its overly "ideal" space that couldn't attribute to any particular style, but "the nature that tolerates all."

1
2 | 3

1. View from the lake
2. Corridor space
3. North elevation

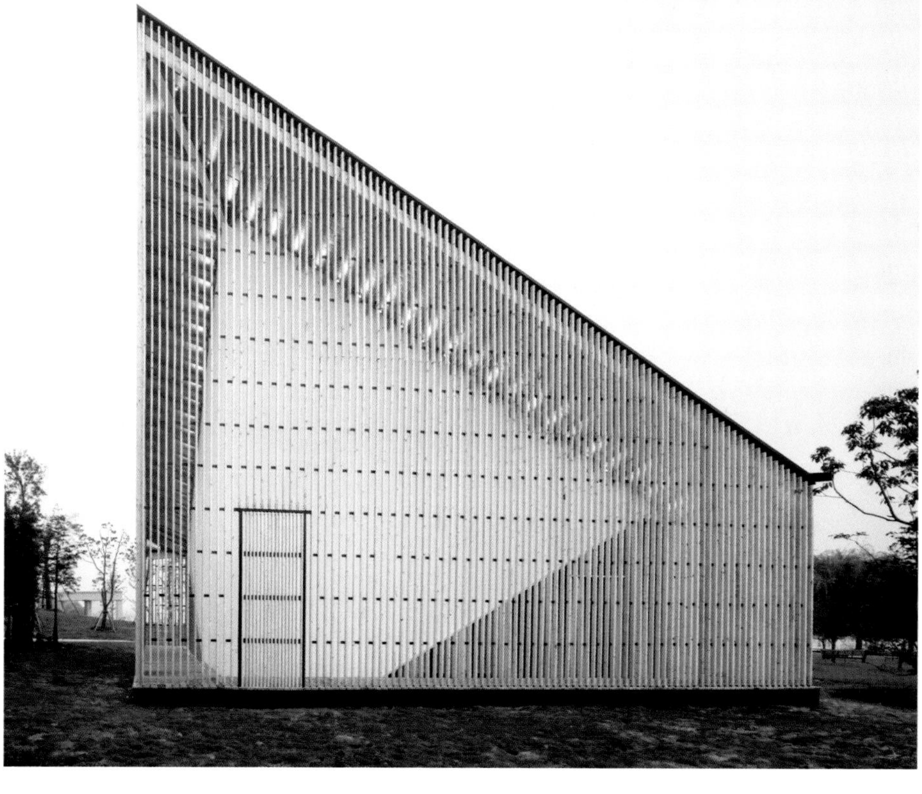

View from the altar

Nave

View toward the ceiling

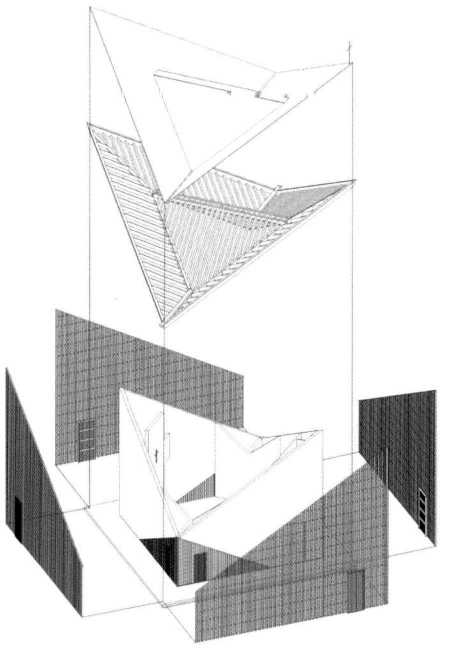
Axonometric diagram

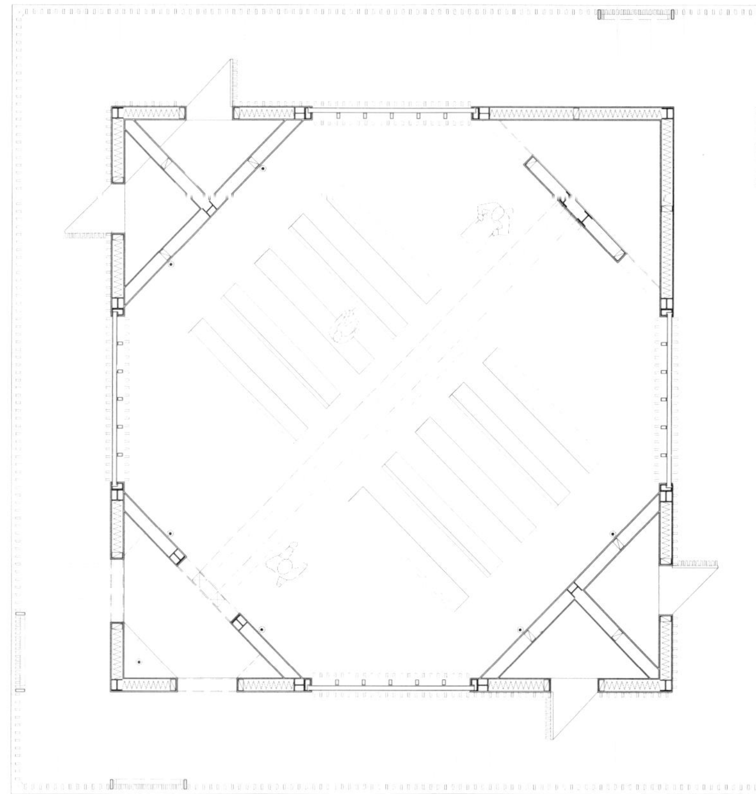
Ground-floor plan

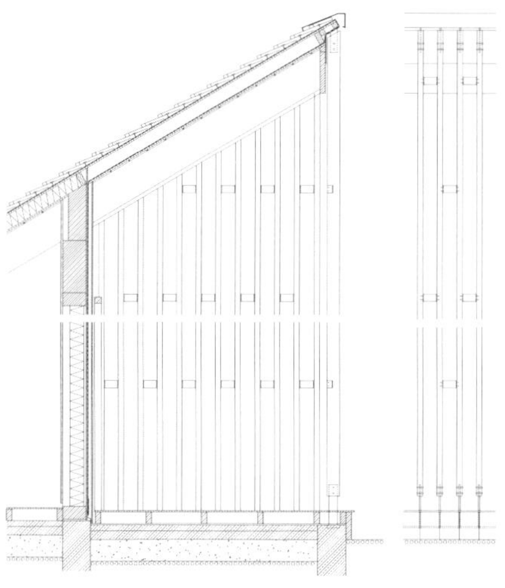
Section detail

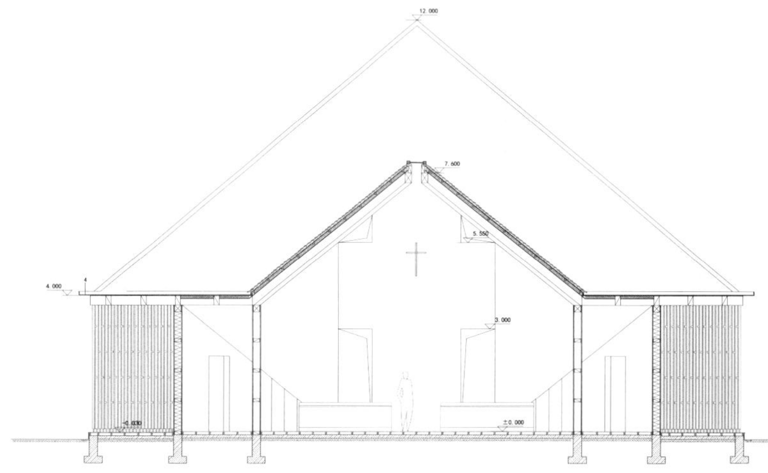

Section

Liu Yichun

Atelier Deshaus
Co-founder and principal architect of Atelier Deshaus
Guest professor at the architecture schools of Tongji University and Southeast University
RIBA Chartered Member
Member, Editorial Board of *The Architect* and *Architectural Journal*

Liu Yichun established Atelier Deshaus together with Chen Yifeng and Zhuang Shen in 2001. Liu has participated in a variety of major international architecture and art exhibitions around the world: Shanghai, Beijing, Hong Kong, Paris, Rotterdam, London, Berlin, Brussels, Lyon, Barcelona, Venice, Prague, Milano, Tokyo, and Vienna. He has also held lectures at many prestigious universities such as the Harvard Graduate School of Design, the University of Hong Kong, Tongji University, Southeast University, the Architectural Institute of France, and École Nationale Supérieure des Beaux-Arts de Lyon, to name a few. His works have been widely published in a number of journals in over twenty-six countries and have won various architectural awards. His design for the Long Museum West Bund was awarded the AR Award for Emerging Architecture by *Architectural Review*, the Honor Award for Architecture Best in Show 2019 by AIA China, and the Golden Prize for Public Architecture at the Architecture Creation Awards of ASC. Atelier Deshaus was recognized as one of ten Design Vanguards in 2011 by *Architectural Record*, as well as the Most Influential Chinese Designer by *Forbes* in 2015, and was also awarded the Architect of the Year 2019 by *Urban Environment Design Magazine*.

Selected Works

2002 Tri-house, Jiangsu, China
2004 The Dongguan Institute of Technology, Dongguan, China
2011 Spiral Gallery I, Shanghai, China
2012 Qingpu Youth Centre, Shanghai, China
2014 Artron (Shanghai) Arts Centre, Shanghai, China
2014 West Bund Art Centre, Shanghai, China
2014 Long Museum West Bund, Shanghai, China
2015 Shanghai Jiading Tao Li Yuan School, Shanghai, China
2015 Blossom Pavilion, Shanghai, China
2015 Atelier Deshaus Office on West Bund, Shanghai, China
2016 Shanghai Modern Art Museum, Shanghai, China
2016 Footbridge on Rihui River, Shanghai, China
2016 Tea House in Li Garden, Shanghai, China
2017 Renovation and Reuse of 80000 Silo Warehouse, Shanghai, China
2018 House ATO, Beijing, China
2018 Golden Ridge Upper-cloister (under construction), Chengde, China
2019 Taizhou Contemporary Art Museum, Taizhou, Zhejiang, China
2019 Qintai Art Museum (under construction), Wuhan, China

1
2

1. Riverside Passage © Tian Fangfang
2. The existing long wall at the site before construction © Atelier Deshaus

Interviewer: Fang Ziyu
Interviewee: Liu Yichun (Liu)
Editor: Mo Wanli

What is your understanding of "building with nature?"

LIU: If we define "nature" as Italian humanist Jacopo Bonfadio did, then there are three kinds: "first nature," or original nature; "second nature," or nature that people have modified for practical purposes, such as agricultural land; and "third nature," which is a state that lies between nature and manufactured environments, for example, ruins reclaimed by nature. Farmlands, arguably, fall within the scope of "building with nature." Some of our recent projects included working with industrial ruins, which I think can also be a kind of "building with nature."

I've only just starting thinking about the phrase "building with nature" and trying to understand these words in conjunction with each other and the work we do. What exists intrinsically is also natural. My master's thesis, written in 1994, was about the design rationale of high-rise buildings and skyscrapers. Ian McHarg's *Design with Nature* was central to my thesis then, and his work remains just as relevant today, although a lot of the focus recently has been on the structural rationale, which relates to the laws of nature. If we look at plant structure, we can question why different species of trees are constrained to different height limitations. Why do animal skeletons collapse when they're enlarged to a certain magnitude? These all come back to the relationship between nature and building.

"Nature" can also mean essence or ferity. In *The Analects of Confucius*, in the adage that espouses a balance of character and cultivation, the Hanzi "*ye*" translates to "nature" and not "wildness." Given that, I'm more inclined to interpret "building with nature" as "building naturally," meaning that we have to comply with existing conditions and unearth their potential. These conditions could be of natural origin, or they could be urban, historical, and cultural conditions. Of course, this also relates to something I had mentioned a great deal recently: causality borrowing propriety situatedness. This perspective leads us to numerous examples of "building with nature," such as the ancient Foguang Temple or the Riverside Passage that Deshaus recently finished renovating.

Blossom Pavilion © Zhou Dingqi

Shanghai Modern Art Museum – structure after renovation © Tian Fangfang

What are the main directions that your practice is currently exploring?

LIU: Being a good architect means succeeding in four interconnected areas: technology, language, lifestyle, and form. One of the more distinct parts of my work recently has been reconstructing the role of existing structures within contemporary Chinese architecture and then thinking about the value of Neue Sachlichkeit (or "new objectivity") created by those structures in relation to their purpose, specifically when they intervene in the design and building process. This direction of thought is related to everything I mentioned earlier; thoughts that sprang from working with industrial architecture and ruins amid all of Shanghai's urban renewal projects in recent years, which I imagine will become more systemic with time.

The previous structure used for coal shipping © Atelier Deshaus

How do you understand the relationship between modern technology and traditional construction?

LIU: This depends on our understanding of "tradition," which includes things tangible and intangible, refined and crude. The mention of "tradition" seemingly brims with connotations of nature. Of course, modern construction technologies are considerably different from traditional ones, but the relationship between architecture and nature is still the same—that is, the relationship between man and nature has always been the same and we can use modern technology to create structures that respect nature.

1
2 | 3

1. Shanghai Modern Art Museum © Tian Fangfang
2-3. Shanghai Modern Art Museum before renovation © Chen Hao

Within the context of globalization, what are the similarities that Chinese architects share with architects from the rest of the world in the way they approach, explore, and practice architecture?

LIU: China's large-scale construction in recent years has already become a major part of global architecture, and the advancements of contemporary Chinese architects over the past two decades speak for itself. Their architectural knowledge and approaches have slowly turned into something unique. We still have to acknowledge that Western countries have a solid cultural foundation when it comes to the study of architecture, but confronting Chinese problems or defining modern Chinese architecture should fall on Chinese architects; so should the exploration and cultural construction of China's architectural history. While some discrepancies are undeniable, we also shouldn't underestimate ourselves. Everyone plays a similar role in creating the future of architecture.

LONG MUSEUM WEST BUND

Location: No. 3398 Longteng Avenue, Shanghai, China
Architect: Atelier Deshaus
Principal architect: Liu Yichun, Chen Yifeng
Design team: Liu Yichun, Chen Yifeng, Wang Longhai, Wang Weishi, Wu Zhenghui, Wang Xuepei, Chen Kun
Gross floor area: 33,070 square meters
Design period: November 2011–July 2012
Completion: March 2014
Photography: Tian Fangfang, Su Shengliang

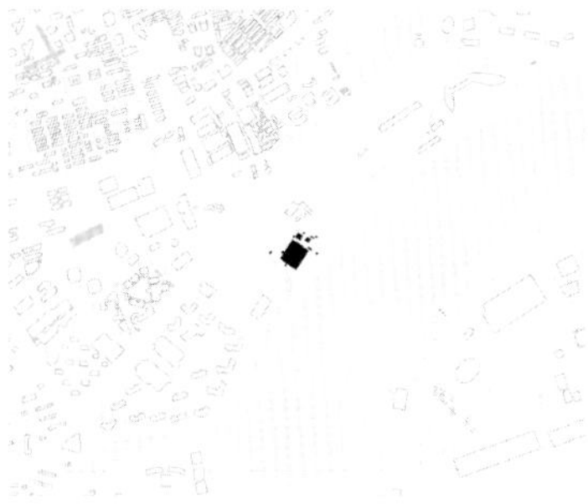

Site plan

Aerial view of the existing site before construction

Old coal-hopper-uploading bridge

Located along the Huangpu River in Shanghai's Xuhui District, the site for the Long Museum West Bund was once a coal dock. At the beginning of the design process, an existing coal-hopper-unloading bridge and a two-story underground parking garage characterized the site. The coal-hopper-bridge was built during the 1950s and is about 110 meters long, 10 meters wide, and 8 meters high. The parking garage had been built two years before the start of the project as part of a building which never materialized.

The new design employs a cantilevered "vault-umbrella" structure. Following a free plan, shear walls were inserted into the basement and connected to the existing column grid, thus transforming the parking garage into a gallery space. Aboveground, the "vault-umbrellas" are connected in different directions, creating multiple interpretations for the space. The technical system of the building is embedded into the hollow space within the "vault-umbrellas." Combined, the "umbrellas" make up a square-shaped site, while simultaneously forming the interior space. The façades of the interior walls and ceilings, both, highlight fair-faced concrete and the angles of the "umbrellas'" geometric boundaries are ambiguous, creating a unique spatial experience that offers both a sense of protection and freedom. With the high-level of integration between the structure, the technical system, and the form's spatial intention, a volumetric structure emerges, echoing the coal-hopper-unloading bridge. Thus, the new building establishes a unique relationship with its site.

Entrance to the museum

Interior

Outdoor space

Between the museum and the revamped coal-hopper-unloading bridge

Vault-umbrella

Ground-floor plan

1. Museum entrance
2. Entrance hall
3. Shop
4. Contemporary art gallery
5. Video room
6. Cloakroom
7. Service room
8. Void
9. Temporary gallery
10. Art and design shop
11. Restaurant
12. VIP room
13. Freight elevator
14. Coal-hopper-uploading-bridge space
15. Artwork by Xu Zhen: *Sports Field*

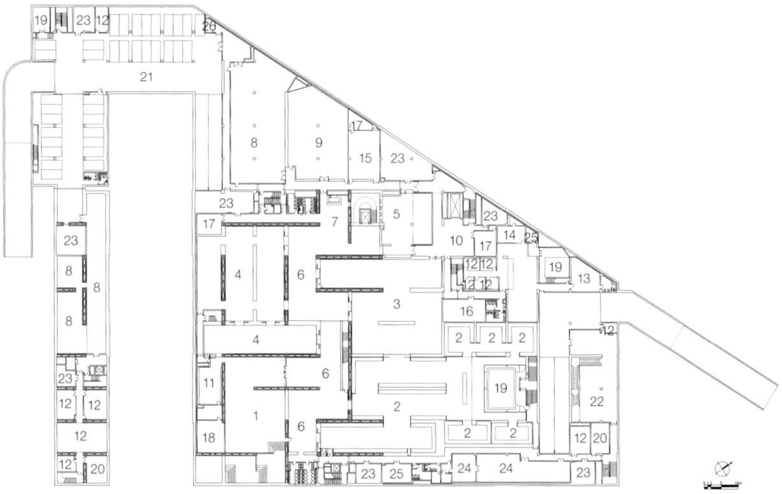

Basement floor plan

1. Contemporary art gallery
2. Ancient art gallery
3. Ancient/modern art gallery
4. Modern art gallery
5. Children's room
6. Corridor
7. Lounge
8. Warehouse
9. Temporary warehouse
10. Uploading area
11. Reading room
12. Office
13. Director's office
14. Meeting room
15. Restoration/studio
16. Archives
17. Archives
18. Storage
19. Courtyard
20. Security/fire control room
21. Parking
22. Bicycle parking
23. HVAC room
24. Substation
25. M&E room

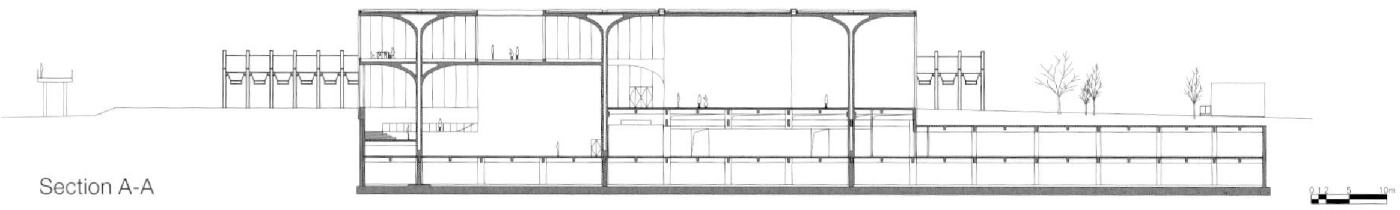

Section A-A

Section model

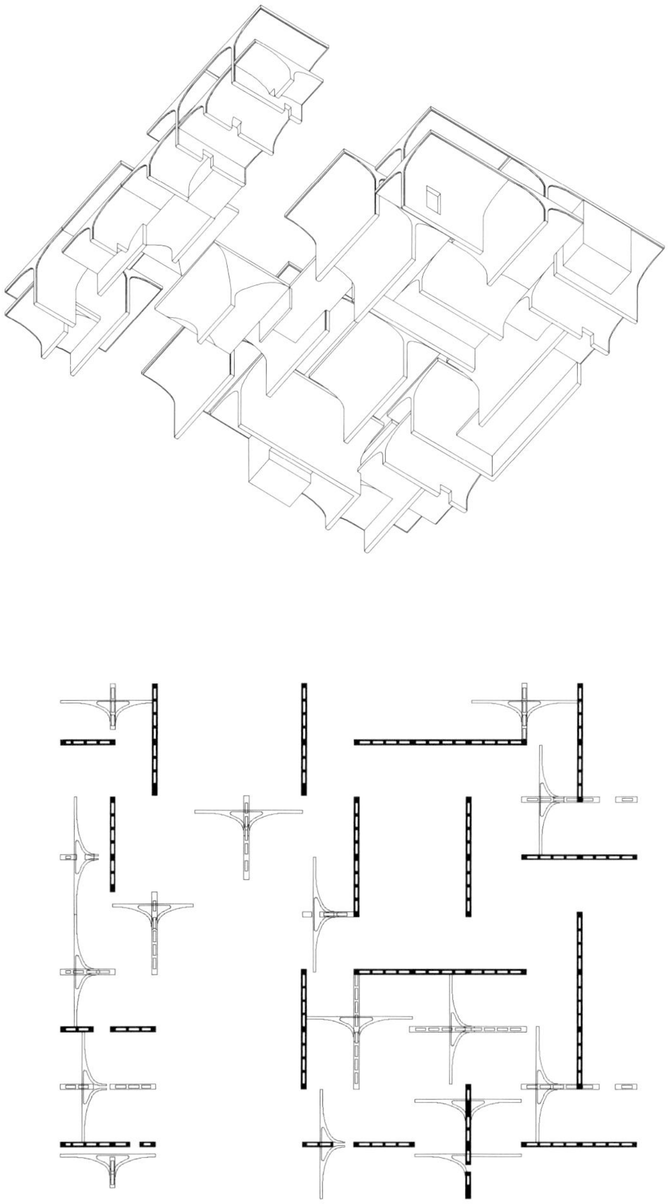

Conceptual isometric and plan drawings

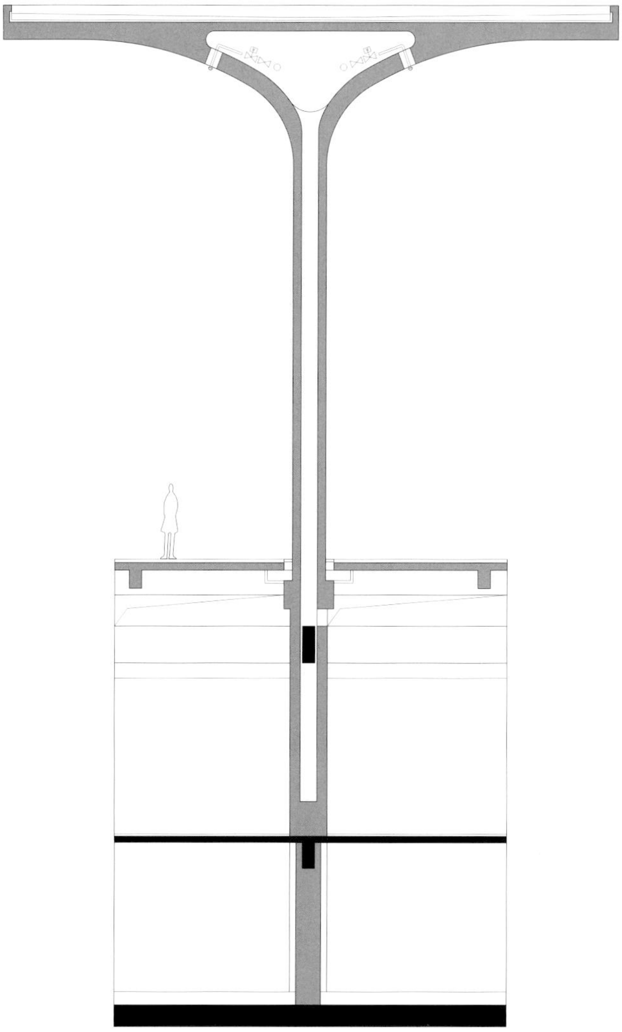

Vault-umbrella detail section

TEA HOUSE IN LI GARDEN

Location: 2555 Longteng Ave, Shanghai, China
Architect: Atelier Deshaus
Principal architect: Liu Yichun, Chen Yifeng
Design team: Shen Wen, Wang Weishi
Structure design team: Zhang Zhun
Landscape design: July-Co Garden
Gross floor area: 19 square meters
Design period: December 2015–April 2016
Completion: 2017
Photography: Tian Fangfang

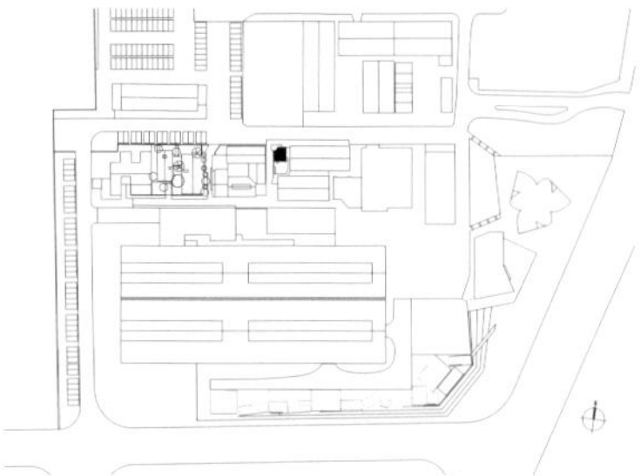

Site plan

Tea House in Li Garden

The Tea House is located in an approximately 110-square-meter garden, canopied under the huge crown of a tall paulownia tree. The garden is also occupied by two staircases connecting to the neighboring office. Thus, minimizing the intervention of the Tea House in the garden was a key point in the design process. The building is placed in the northwest corner where the paulownia tree stands, by the back wall. Its high crown and thick trunk measuring 90 centimeters in diameter become essential spatial components. With the enclosure of the back wall, the yard space behind the Tea House becomes involved with the interior, thus further reducing the volume of the Tea House itself.

Another important spatial intention is to minimize the footprint of the Tea House. We sought to achieve this through three layers of cantilevered plates at different heights. The one that is 45 centimeters high works as a bench encircling the building, defining the upper parts as the inside and the lower parts as the outside; the one set at 1.8 meters extends through the interior space. At the same time, the exterior eaves gallery does not bother other activities. The roof is the last cantilever, redefining diverse outer space on the south, the north, and the west. It covers an area of 40 square meters with a ground floor of only 19 square meters. The roof plate extending in different directions also strengthens the spatial interaction between the Tea House and the garden.

Vertical and horizontal structural components are designed to be as thin as possible. We choose to use 60-by-60-millimeter square steel in the whole building. In addition to satisfying the structural requirement, the square steel is also part of the formal composition. It is the structural element and also adapts itself to the scale of the furniture, thus establishing a close relationship with human body.

The roof is made of an 8-millimeter-thick steel board. Its insulation board is fixed by anti-ribbed steel panels to keep the roof smooth. Considering the lighting system and thermal insulation, we made a suspended ceiling that hides the structural beams, and also place the air-conditioning system under the floor.

The Tea House

Structure detail

Space, furniture, and scale

Three layers of cantilevered plates in the Tea House

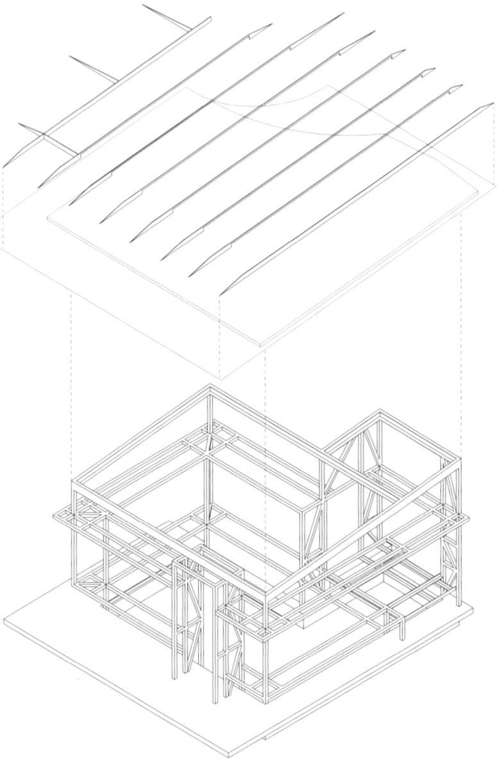

Structural diagram

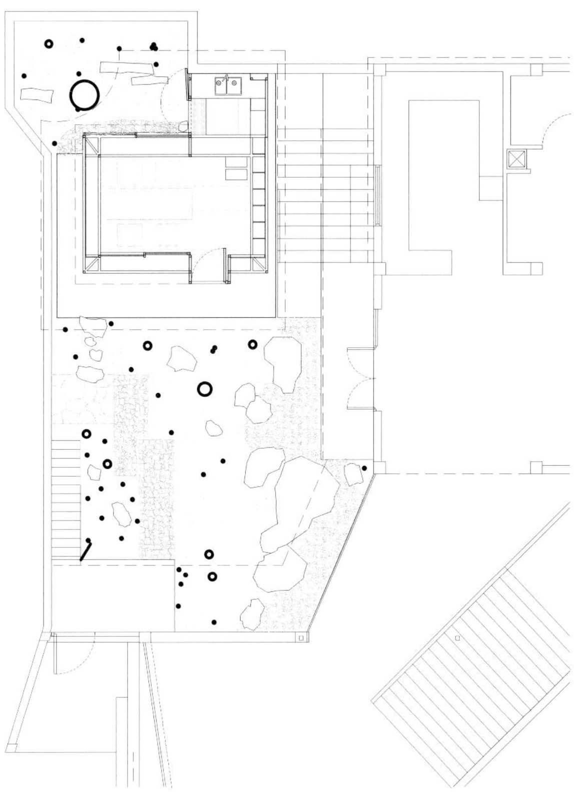

Floor plan

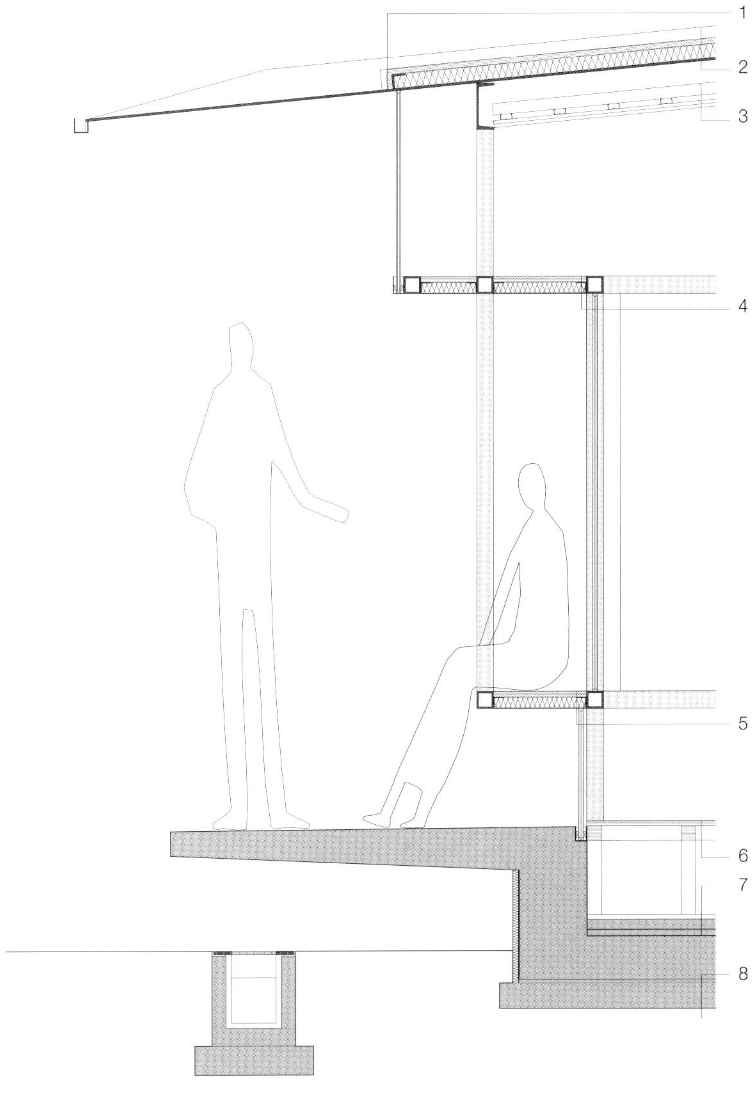

Wall detail

1. Waterproof membrane (sealant on edges)
2. High polymer asphalt waterproof membrane
   18 mm laminated plywood board
   L50 angle steel rib
   (50 mm thermal insulation)
   8 mm structural steel plate
3. 9 mm double-layer paper-faced gypsum board suspended ceiling
   waterproof membrane (sealant on edges)
   white paint
4. 20 mm elm board
   40 mm thermal insulation
   1.5 mm steel plate
   black metal paint
   L35 connector
5. 20 mm elm board
   40 mm thermal insulation
   1.5 mm steel plate
   black metal paint
   L35 connector
6. Multi-ply solid wood parquet flooring
   50x50 mm wood joist, 200 mm elevated with antiseptic
   paint on surface
7. 15 mm 1:2.5 cement mortar
   Q.S. cement flour spread on surface, leveled
   35 mm C20 fine aggregate concrete
   1.5 mm polyurethane (PU) waterproof layer
   at least 20 mm 1:3 cement mortar slope-making layer, leveled
   cement mortar (construction glue doped), single layer
   1.5 mm polyurethane (PU) waterproof layer
   reinforced-concrete slab
8. Isolation layer
   high polymer asphalt waterproof membrane
   20 mm 1:2.5 cement mortar
   100 mm C15 concrete bedding
   rammed earth

EXPLORATION AWARD IN TECHNOLOGY

The Exploration Award in Technology focuses on projects with a humanistic spirit and those that show continuous innovation with architectural technologies through two or more high-quality works created in recent years. The award also encourages cross-professional and cross-disciplinary exploration.

Luo Yujie
LUO Studio

Laureate

Li Xinggang
Atelier Li Xinggang

Shortlisted

Philip F. Yuan
Archi-Union Architects

Shortlisted

Luo Yujie

LUO Studio
Founder and principal architect of LUO studio

LUO studio is committed to creating durable, friendly, high-quality spaces through creative thinking, the spirit of craftsmanship, and the principle of caring for nature. The studio's exceptional works have been shortlisted and awarded with numerous design awards worldwide. These include the 2019 WAN Award for Wood in Architecture (Gold Winner), the 2019 ABB LEAF Award for Best Achievement in Environmental Performance (winner), the 2019 International Design Media Award Annual Exhibition Space Award (winner), the 2019 AR Emerging Architecture Awards (shortlisted), the 2019 A+ Awards for Concepts+Architecture+Technology (finalist), the Technological Innovation Award of the 2018 WA Awards for Chinese Architecture (shortlisted), and *Dezeen*'s Top 10 Chinese Architecture Projects of 2018.

Selected Works

2010 Concierge of Ministry of Commerce of the People's Republic of China, Beijing, China
2013 Architect's Working Desk "3in1," Beijing, China
2013 Karamay Science Museum, Xinjiang, China
2014 Changde Planning Exhibition Hall, Changchun, China
2015 Installation Work "The Constant," Beijing, China
2017 Shading Device in South Area of TaiKoo Li Sanlitun, Beijing, China
2017 9.639 — An Inserted Variable Office, Beijing, China
2017 Shagezhai Stage, Henan, China
2017 People's Stage in Shagezhai Village, Henan, China
2018 Longfu Life Experience Center, Henan, China
2018 Children's House in Dong'anshang Village, Henan, China
2018 Pergola in Luotuowan Village, Hebei, China
2019 Temporary Site of Shengli Market, Henan, China
2019 Shared Lady Beetle — A Micro Movable Library for Kids, Beijing, China
2019 Dongsheng No. 6 Middle School, Ordos, China
2019 Party and Community Center of Yuanheguan Village, Wudang Mountain Tourism Economic Zone, China
2019 Natural Book House in Zheshui Village, Lingchuan County, China

1
2

1. Pergola in Luotuowan Village © Jin Weiqi
2. Kids playing under the Pergola in Luotuowan Village © Jin Weiqi

Interviewer: Fang Ziyu
Interviewee: Luo Yujie (Luo)
Editor: Mo Wanli

What is your understanding of "building with nature?"

LUO: I think it's a kind of natural construction—one that returns to the true, fundamental, unpretentious method of building in architecture, such as rural houses, like the traditional structures described in *Yingzhao Fashi*, a technical treatise on architecture and craftsmanship written in the Song dynasty, the Fujian tulou roundhouses, and the stilt-style architecture in the south. All of these can be considered "building with nature," based on the local climate and materials. The most durable, most comfortable buildings best suited to the locality are made for more than just form.

What are the main directions that your practice is currently exploring?

LUO: I'm exploring sustainable steel and wood construction. More broadly speaking, sustainable technology and construction. Focusing on the construction itself means creating larger, more durable, more flexible spaces with the least amount of materials. I hope that my exploration will offer more creative solutions to some of our architectural problems, like the waste of materials, or buildings that are demolished because of limitations in their use. My efforts are certainly not the only solution, but they offer one possibility. Through

Temporary Site of Shengli Market © Jin Weiqi

the Longfu Life Experience Center, I was able to reflect on construction waste. Given that sales offices like that are used only for a short amount of time before being demolished, could relatively affordable and reusable materials be used instead toward creating a module-based structure that could be moved and reassembled? That would expand possibilities of future use and growth.

Exploring sustainability has been central to my thoughts. Although I didn't necessarily set myself up for this from the start, I have always wanted to preserve resources and build locally. That general direction grew clearer during my practice. My explorations in steel and wood construction started with the pergola in Luotuowan Village, my first project after leaving a large design institute and one that used discarded materials to achieve sustainability. After, both the People's Stage in Shagezhai Village and the Longfu Life Experience Center gradually became a part of my thoughts when thinking about the future possibilities of a space. This was similar to the idea of "total space" espoused by Ludwig Mies van der Rohe when he was designing S. R. Crown Hall at the Illinois Institute of Technology. I want there to be a weak tie between space and function; that way, buildings can immediately adapt to change. This also enables ease in demolishing and reassembling a structure, as well as allows the possibility of expanding it. For instance, could we feasibly enlarge a space by growing it and adding to it, rather than taking it down and replacing it? That's why I identify to some extent with the ideas of Japan's Metabolism movement.

Going back to the example of Longfu Life Experience Center—the owner later turned it into an activity space on a farm by disassembling and reorganizing the structure's modular units, along with the moveable buried steel foundation. Those qualities facilitated the moving of the structure between the two sites. The modules can also be recycled later if the structure is no longer needed; I can even take four of them back and reassemble them into a studio for myself. I now even have my own workshop to conduct further research on wooden materials and structures.

What are the biggest challenges in your exploration of steel and wood construction?

LUO: The suitability of technology in extreme conditions, like severe winters or barrenness. Most of the time, steel and wood structures create a space that isn't suited for all environments. That is why we are exploring how they can be integrated with other materials, like raw earth, bricks, and concrete, to help maintain the structure.

1
2

1. Natural Book House in Zheshui Village © Jin Weiqi
2. Inside the Natural Book House © Jin Weiqi

How do you view the traditional Chinese timber construction system and your explorations of design?

LUO: I would never deliberately cater to traditional construction, but the things I see around me undoubtedly leave an impression that might unconsciously reappear in my work. In delving deeper into my practice, I'm slowly realizing the relationship between my work and traditional construction, which allows me to conduct related studies. I'm working on one right now about the construction logic of timber structure systems in rural architecture and its contemporary practical exploration. Along the way, I've slowly built an interest in learning more about traditional construction. This interest is more about the structural rationale of traditional buildings and less about their appearance. For instance, when I was at a village in Lishui, Zhejiang, I saw an assembled, movable, traditional wood-frame barn. Its style was influenced by the traditional Chuan-Dou columns-and-tie style of architecture, yet its enclosure featured the Jinggan log cabin style. I was pleasantly surprised to see individual structures transcend their usual paradigms but still end up well-constructed.

LONGFU LIFE EXPERIENCE CENTER

Location: Puyang County, Henan Province, China
Architect: LUO Studio
Principal architect: Luo Yujie
Design team: Wang Xiaotao, Wei Wenjing
Gross floor area: 1,590 square meters
Completion: April 2018
Photography: Jin Weiqi

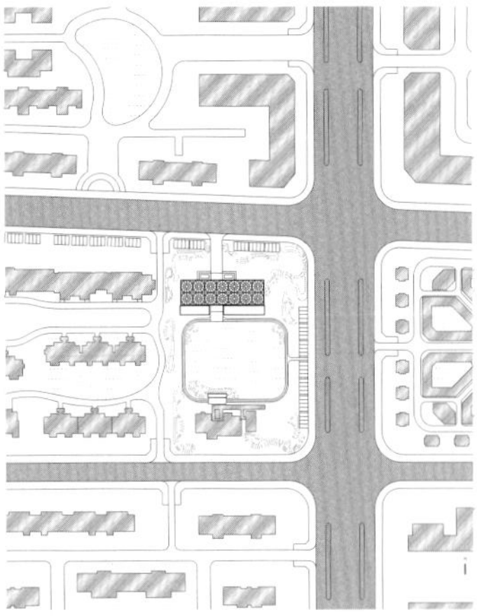
Site plan

Longfu Life Experience Center at night

Most real estate sales centers are highly temporary structures that are torn down at the end of sales for the corresponding real estate project. This project starts from creating a space that both fulfills its temporary sales function and provides the possibility of greater, extended use. The client was a landowner with a high degree of quality control over the property development, and hoped to convey the idea of an eco-friendly experience through the sales center. Timber was without a doubt the optimal construction material. As an eco-friendly material, it creates a connection to nature.

We purchased highly cost-effective, conventional, squared timber measuring 3 meters, 4 meters, and 6 meters in length with a cross-section of about 200 millimeters. The design task was to create an expansive, diversified, multifunctional space from this uniform timber. Using single wooden pillars as a standalone supporting unit would not suffice because we would not be able to achieve a free-standing effect for the building. Instead, it was more suitable to combine a number of timber pillars to form clustered columns. Based on a number of factors, like the cross-sectional dimensions of the pillars, the appropriate height, and a convenient construction space, we determined that the shape of a standard unit would be sub-rounded and made of twelve-sided clustered columns. They would measure 1 meter across at the diameter with the wooden beam's cross-section at 120 by 180 millimeters. Shaped like trees, the vertical modules are divided into five segments measuring about 2 meters each. They expand upward and outward, eventually forming a bounded space reaching 4.5 meters in height and 8 meters across each body.

The bottom part of the clustered columns forms a polygon. To close the gap between each independent connector, they stretch upward and shift from a sub-rounded shape into a squared space. The modules intertwine horizontally and longitudinally. Like Lego bricks, the modules can be independent or combined with others to create the needed dimensions. The connected modules also form a continuous arch, which provides a highly stable load-bearing structure. Each extension only makes the building more stable.

Due to the project's circumstances, we were tasked with completing the design, construction, and decoration in less than two months, all while containing costs. The building also needed to be constructed and deconstructed quickly, as well as reusable. These conditions presented both major challenges and restrictions to the team.

Façade

Interior atrium

Our strategy was as follows:

1. Use the most basic construction methods and the most common material processing techniques. This allowed for ordinary workers to participate in the construction, and for materials to be processed in common factories.

2. Standardize and modularize as much as possible. We broke down the entire structure into individual construction units and then broke those down into standardized pieces. In the end, each unit could be built using only three basic components, which controlled the size of the basic units. With that, we established a unified, clean assemblage process.

3. We subdivided all possible work, strove to assign processing across different factories, and arranged production workshops. We reallocated equipment, space, and distance as needed. All of the materials and components could be used interchangeably in subsequent tasks along the building process, rather than be held up at the construction site idle waiting for preceding tasks to be completed. These strategies enabled us to finish construction and soft installation within forty-nine days and ahead of schedule.

Out of consideration for its varied use, we laid the ground-floor area with cement mortar. Other than that, all other components were connected with bolts, making it easy to take down and reinstall. In turn, this becomes a "longevity" structure that can be completely moved and reused, taking on a state of reversible construction.

The furniture, equipment, electromechanics, pipelines, and exterior were all integrated into the structural units or the overall structure itself. The core structural trees naturally "produce" furniture, fences, and an outward-weaving exterior. At the same time, these necessary components are borne out of the main structure and thus respond in synergy with the structure, lending it greater stability.

Longfu Life Experience Center uses conventional, standardized timber found domestically, as well as common processing and construction methods in order to create infinite possibilities for its uses. Built upon a foundation of "universal uses," the space remains constant but can adapt to different times or uses. Modules, or the entire structure can be expanded, reduced, replaced, or moved. It can also be taken down completely. Through its reversible construction, its materials can be returned to their original condition and used in other construction projects. This achieves the optimal possibilities of "universal use" for both the space and materials.

Close-up view of the wooden columns

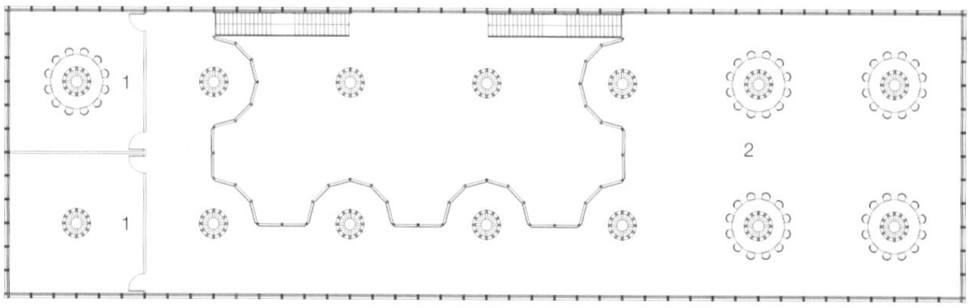

Second-floor plan

1. Office
2. Kids' zone

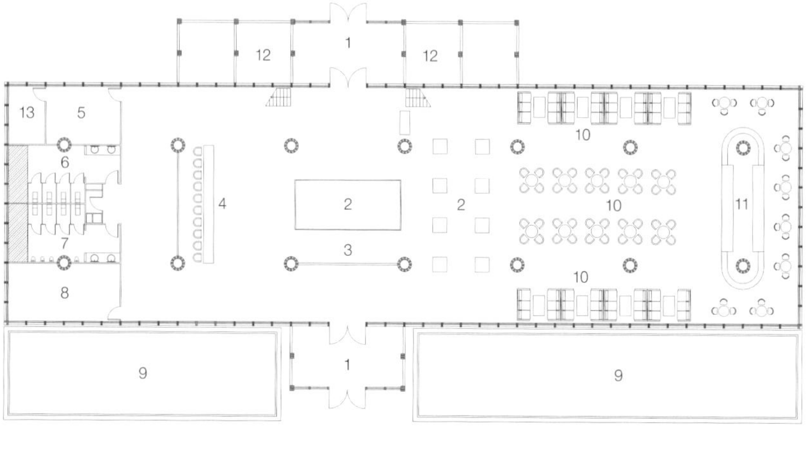

Ground-floor plan

1. Lobby
2. Model display area
3. Multimedia display area
4. Reception area
5. Distribution room
6. Women's restroom
7. Men's restroom
8. Office
9. Mirror pool
10. Negotiation area
11. Water bar
12. Planting region
13. Storage room

Kids' zone

Single-unit tree house

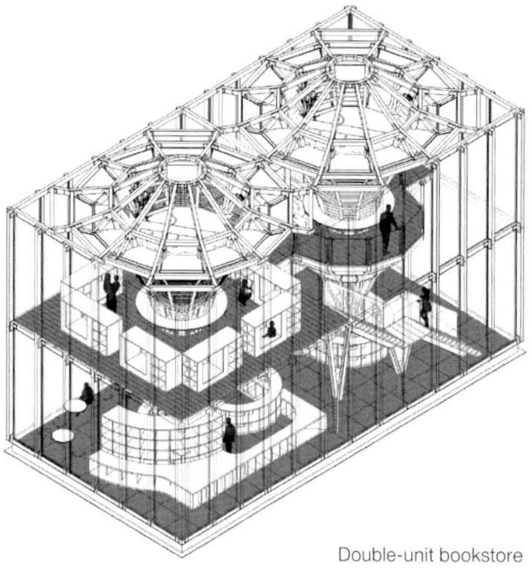

Double-unit bookstore

4-unit for workspace

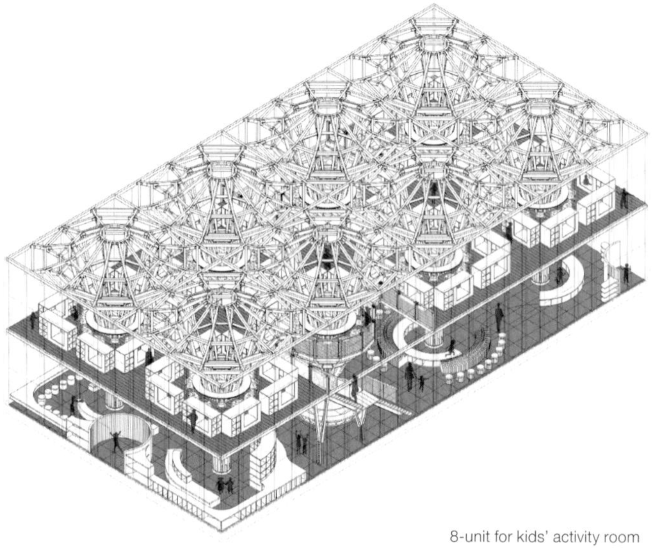

8-unit for kids' activity room

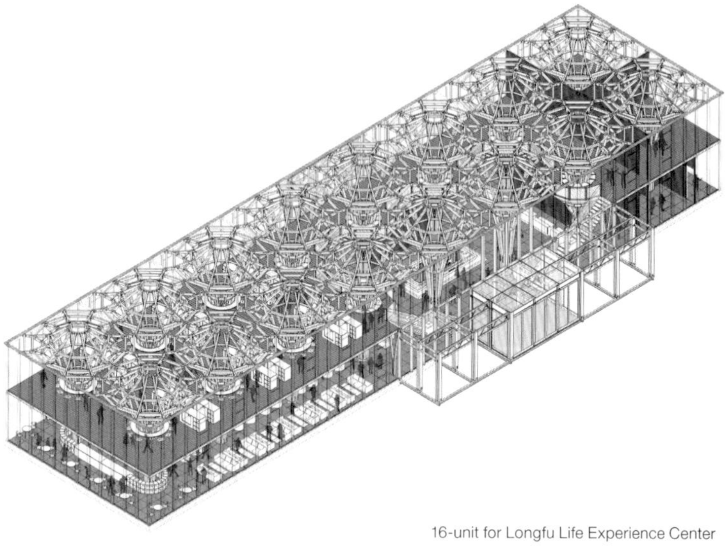

16-unit for Longfu Life Experience Center

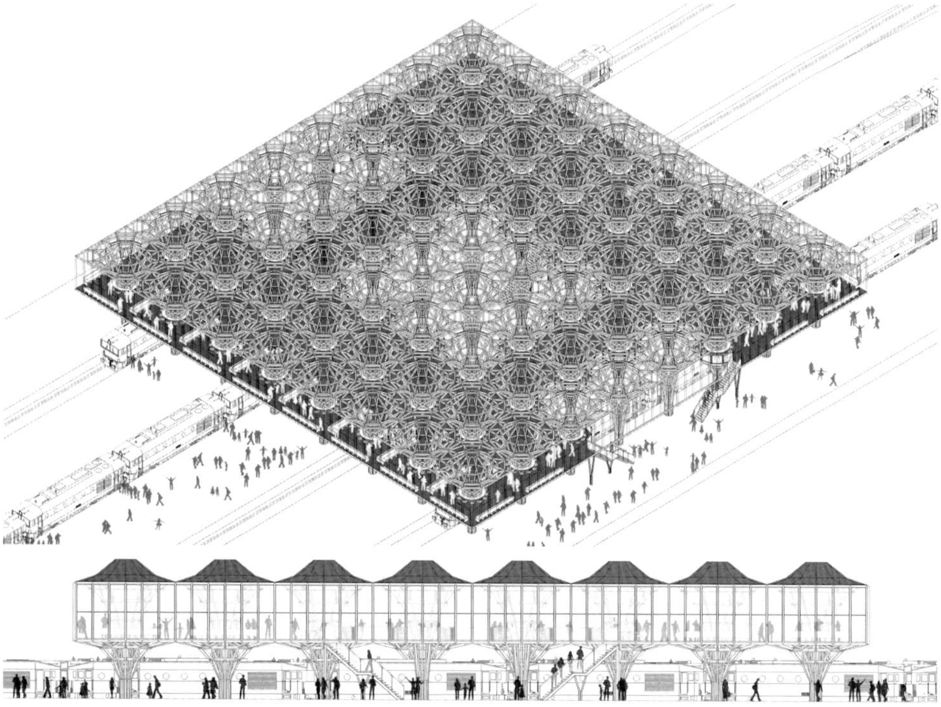

64-unit for a transit hub

Unit program study

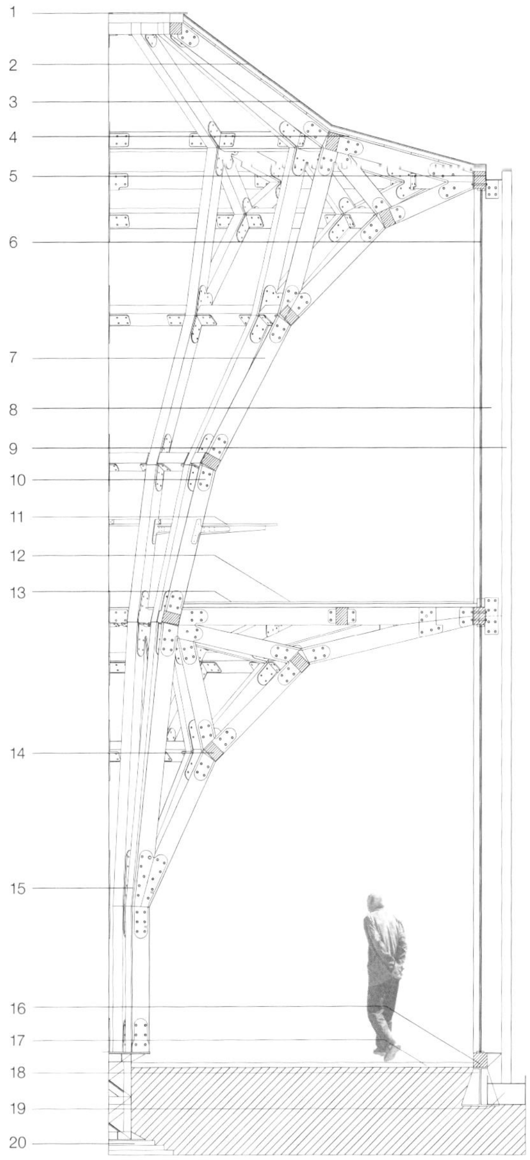

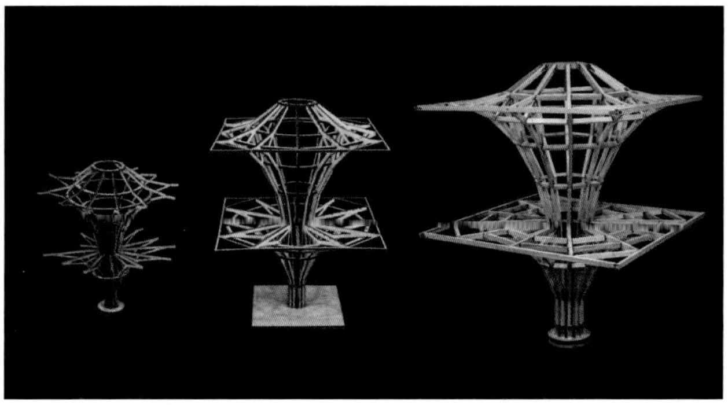

Structure model

Structural unit detail

1. 8 mm + 8 mm double toughened laminated glass
2. 3 mm asphalt waterproof rolling material
3. 10 mm bamboo veneer
4. 25 mm anticorrosion board
5. 3 mm carbon-steel rain gutter
6. 6 mm + 9 mm + 6 mm tempered insulating glass
7. 120x180 mm anticorrosive wood
8. 120x300 mm anticorrosive wood
9. 120x100x3 mm downspouts
10. 10 mm steel joint member
11. 30 mm desktop board
12. 15 mm wood floor
13. 40 mm anticorrosive wood
14. 120x120 mm anticorrosive wood columns
15. 10 mm steel ring members
16. 150x150 mm embalming log
17. 800x800 mm marble tile
18. H-shaped steel foundation
19. 3 mm carbon-steel rain gutter
20. 50-mm-thick steel plate base

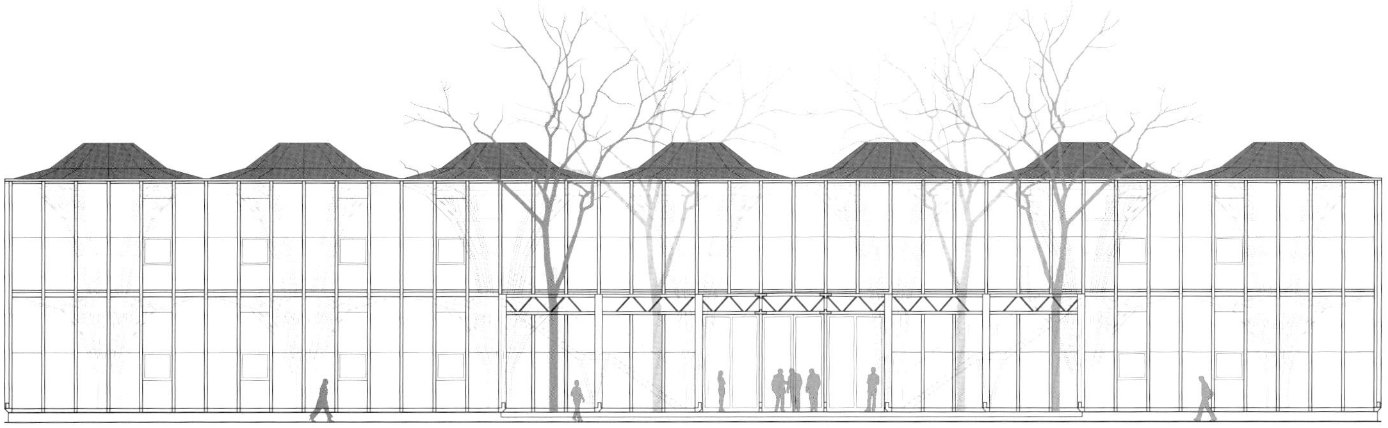

Elevation

YUANHEGUAN VILLAGE COMMUNITY CENTER

Location: Yuanheguan Village, Wudang Mountains Tourism and Special Economic Zone, Danjiangkou, Shiyan City, Hubei Province, China
Architect: LUO Studio
Principal architect: Luo Yujie
Design team: Wei Wenjing
Gross floor area: 545 square meters
Design period: October 2019
Construction period: October 2019–December 2019
Completion: December 2019
Photography: Jin Weiqi

Site plan

Aerial view

Yuanheguan Village Community Center: A Structure Featuring Successive Growth

In the Wudang Mountains Tourism and Special Economic Zone, a commercial model for homestays is being actively promoted with the surrounding scenic area being overhauled accordingly. Situated close to the entrance of the scenic area, Yuanheguan Village was prioritized for the pilot project. The plan was to transform this previous location of the village committee into a model bed and breakfast area, and so, the construction of a new community center and the relocation of the village committee quickly became of utmost importance. The new site, a long abandoned homestead, lies adjacent to the village's main road. A foundation, as well as structural columns on the ground floor had previously been built on the plot, and continuing construction on these existing structures would save time significantly.

Construction Logic: Building Wooden Extensions Atop the Concrete Columns

Subsequent construction progressed along three phases.

Adding wooden columns to the first level and organizing the grid: the existing concrete columns on the site made up a grid, but it was an irregular one. Four rows of columns were laid in a south–north orientation with a distance of 5.75, 2, and 6.5 meters, respectively, between them. The columns along the east–west axis on the north side were either 4.15 or 4.25 meters apart, while the three different spans of the south were 2.6, 3.5, and 3.6 meters, causing an irregularity in the center of the column grid. In order to account for this incomplete concrete column grid and the generally lower span of wooden beams, columns needed to be added in the center of the grid. By connecting the new timber columns to the old concrete ones with wooden beams, LUO studio integrated the concrete columns of the ground floor with the upper timber structure.

Entrance to the community center

An upward-growing structure: starting from the ground-floor beam and column structure, the project keeps extending upwards. The concrete columns have a cross-section of 450 by 450 millimeters, which proved too large for wooden materials. Therefore, four 150-by-150-millimeter wooden pillars were bundled together to form a clustered column, which also facilitated the intersection and connection of the beams and columns. With its density of columns and beams spaced 2 meters apart, the central part of the ground-floor grid was raised to create the roof ridge including a linear skylight. This allows abundant daylight to enter the entire 15-meter-wide space. The roof slopes to the northern and southern sides while the entrance lies on the north side facing the street. Large overhead eaves form a covered area that reflects the characteristics of the local architecture unique to the region around the Wudang Mountains. Set on the south side of the second floor, a terrace opens to a view of the distant mountains, the nearby Taoist temple, and the main village area.

Filling in horizontal and vertical partitions and enclosures: after the main structure was completed, the next steps were filling in the exterior walls, partitioning the interior spaces, and adding floor slabs. To prevent a stark visual disruption with the surrounding buildings, the ground floor mainly applies masonry walls. The walls feature an even mix of gray bricks and glass bricks that ensure ample daylight enters the internal space.

On the second floor, large floor-to-ceiling windows provide immersive views of the outside. The dense central columns define the northern and southern areas of the interior space. The northern part is an open public area while the southern area serves as a workspace and a space to hold meetings. The central area between the northern and southern zones is relatively narrow, but manages to still comfortably host the staircases and restrooms. In order to provide ample natural light for the office and service spaces on the ground floor, an opening was carved into the northern side of the second floor, allowing light to reach the bottom of the building. Due to height limitations, the mezzanine on the third floor is mainly set up in the central area and will be used as storage space.

1 | 2
3 | 4

1. View toward the upper floor
2. View of the sitting area
3. Existing concrete columns
4. Wooden beams added to the existing concrete columns

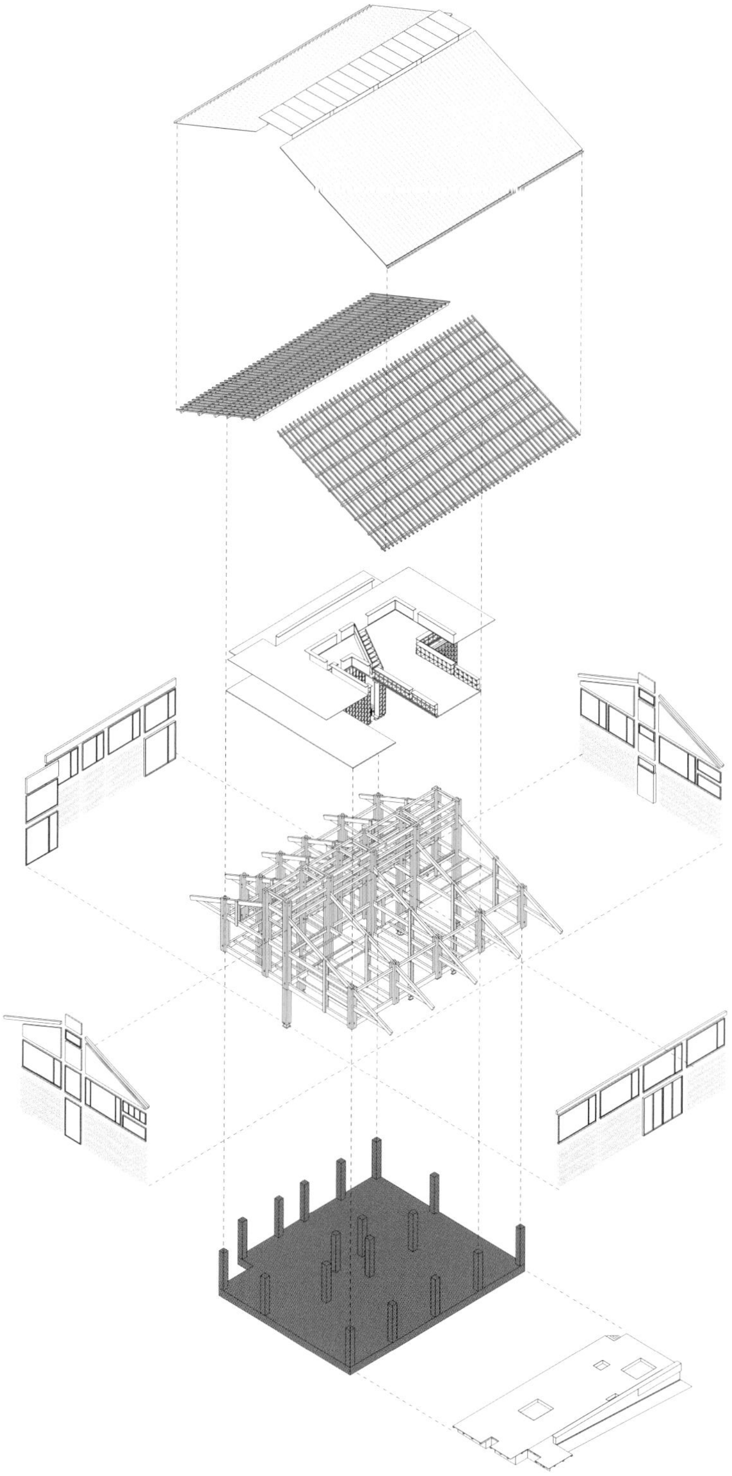

Axonometric diagram

Fast Construction Measures

Due to the speedy construction and development of the bed and breakfast area, the new village office had to be built within two months, presenting a momentous challenge to the designers and the construction team. Thus three measures were taken.

1. Overall design and construction arrangements: Because of the tight schedule, design and construction work started almost simultaneously. To ensure high-efficiency, drawings were produced according to single construction steps. In addition, the designers stayed on-site the entire time to support the construction work. They were able to elucidate specific parts of the process and thus simplify the drawing work, as well as resolve any issues on the spot so as to keep construction going.

2. The principle of prefabricated construction: Factory-made materials were the first choice. By preparing ahead all the materials that would be needed later in the construction, the team was able to keep on-site work focused on installation and assembly.

3. Minimizing use of non-standard parts: Even though the original concrete column grid was very irregular, LUO Studio adopted various methods of reorganizing the grid to standardize the structural elements, doors, windows, and other components for the subsequent construction process. In order to reduce the material consumption caused by cutting, the design and arrangement of construction parts were also guided by common industrial sizes.

Li Xinggang

Atelier Li Xinggang
Founder and principal architect of Atelier Li Xinggang

Founded by Li Xinggang in 2003, Atelier Li Xinggang advocates the process of "research + design," and emphasizes the reaction of architecture to context, nature, site, material, and user. The studio focuses on complete designs that include the control of the buildings, and their interiors, and landscapes. Thus, they approach contemporary architectural works with a cultural depth and aesthetic affection. The atelier also launched a series of studies, such as *Chinese Gardens – Settlements* and *Reading Masters*. The practice of Atelier Li Xinggang has been honored with design awards including the ARCASIA Gold Award for Architecture (2019), the World Architecture Awards for Chinese Architecture (2014/2016/2018), the ArchDaily Building of Year Award (2018), and the National Excellent Engineering Investigation and Design Gold and Silver Awards (2009/2000/2010). Li has also received the China Youth Science and Technology Award (2007) and the esteemed National Engineering Survey and Design Master Award (2016).

Selected Works

2002 Xingtao Residential Quarter (Phase 1), Beijing, China
2001 Teda Primary School, Tianjin, China
2001 Xingtao Reception and Exhibition Center, Beijing, China
2006 Daxing Culture Centre, Beijing, China
2007 Renovation of No. B-59-1, Fuxing Road, Beijing, China
2008 Paper-brick House, Venice, Italy
2008 Xihuan Plaza and Xizhimen Transportation Exchange Hub (in partnership with AREP, France), Beijing, China
2008 The National Stadium–the Main Stadium of the 2008 Olympic Games (in partnership with Herzog & de Meuron Architects), Beijing, China
2010 Hi-land Mingzuo, Weihai, China
2010 Jianchuan Mirror Museum and Wenchuan Earthquake Memorial, Anren, China
2010 Accesses and subsidiaries of Line 4 & Daxing Line of Beijing Subway, Beijing, China
2010 Xi'erqi Station of Changping Line of Beijing Subway, Beijing, China
2011 Hainan International Conference and Exhibition Center, Haikou, China
2011 Entrance to Site of Xanadu, Inner Mongolia, China
2012 Xibaipo China Resources Hope Town, Hebei, China
2013 Jixi Museum, Jixi, China
2014 China Custom Museum, Beijing, China
2015 Bird's Nest Culture Center, Beijing, China
2015 The Third Space Complex, Tangshan, China
2015 Shangqiu Museum, Shangqiu, China
2015 Main Accreditation Centre of IAAF World Championships Beijing 2015, Beijing, China
2015 Gymnasium of the New Campus of Tianjin University, Tianjin, China
2015 Museum at Site of Xanadu, Inner Mongolia, China
2016 Chaoyang District Incineration Center of Domestic Waste Comprehensive Treatment Plant, Beijing, China
2017 Renovation of No. 28 Dayuan HuTong, Beijing, China
2017 Camp Service Center in Louna, Xingyi, China
2018 Holiday Inn Express Beijing shougang Silo-pavilion, Beijing, China

Jixi Museum © Qiu Jianbing

Entrance to Site of Xanadu © Zhang Guangyuan

Interviewer: Fang Ziyu
Interviewee: Li Xinggang (Li)
Editor: Mo Wanli

What is your understanding of "building with nature?"

LI: In my opinion, it means: natural, of itself, or responding to real-life conditions, including the environment, construction backgrounds, technology and the needs of future users. It means finding opportunities and entry points for design within these conditions, rather than creating a certain subjective imaginary state of architecture. "Natural" also links directly to the notion of nature, therefore, one of the aspects of "building with nature" in everyday urban architecture is to explore the relationship between architecture and nature.

What are the main directions that your practice is currently exploring?

LI: "Poetic scene and integrated geometry" is a design approach that I have formed and refined in my practice in recent years. At its core, it explores architecture that interacts with nature. "Integrated geometry" relates to the building itself—the basis for the interactions and transformations of structure, space, form, and so forth. It provides the building with a concise order and an interface that can capture poetic scenes, thus reflecting a manufactured essence and materiality. "Poetic scene," on the other hand, points to an indispensable spatial poetry closely related to nature—a profound scene that is constantly induced by artificial interfaces and presented to people, thus reflecting both naturality and spirituality. "Poetic scene" is achieved through "integrated geometry," while the building itself is used to create spatial poetry. The physical "integrated geometry" and the metaphysical "poetic scene" are the cause and effect of each other, and at last integrated geometry is transformed into a poetic scene. In the end, it is about creating an interplay between the artificial and the natural; the integrated entity they form becomes the ideal building and the ideal world in the life of its users. For example, the entrance to Xanadu Park is a group of small communities on the grasslands, while the gymnasium of the New Campus of Tianjin University adopts a set of "structural communities" to establish an identifiable sense of place in an otherwise featureless site, and to pursue the right relation between structure, space, and the scale of moving human bodies. The Hainan International Convention and Exhibition Center, on the other hand, forms a large space through its structural units, which simultaneously dissolve the scale of the large space and make it more intimate. In this sense, it is similar to the spatial scale of the Tianjin University gymnasium's interior.

How do you understand the relationship between architecture and technology?

LI: I think that technology serves the creation of good architecture and is an important part of thinking about architecture as a whole. Nonetheless, it shouldn't be defined or discussed in isolation. For me, technology is relatively secondary, or at most, one part of a broader consideration. It should not be a prerequisite. I won't design a building which cannot be technologically realized. The new Tianjin University gymnasium, while recognized as being representative of technological exploration, still uses conventional technologies such as concrete, and a thin shell structure. The choice of this structure or technology comes from the spatial scale of the gymnasium and how appropriate it is for the design. It's not a deliberate technical exploration.

In my opinion, perhaps "appropriateness" is a more fitting word than "exploration." The latter defines the value of technology in a particularized, easily misleading way, as if only sophisticated and unprecedented technologies are deemed good. Architecture should not follow technology. Architecture needs to care for people's lives comprehensively, and the physical and mental comfort that the users feel in their lives is not necessarily related to whether the building is constructed with advanced technology or not.

THE SITE OF XANADU MUSEUM

Location: Zhenglan Banner, Inner Mongolia Autonomous Region, China
Architect: Atelier Li Xinggang
Principal architect: Li Xinggang
Design team: Tan Zeyang, Fu Bangbao, Zhao Xiaoyu
Structure design team: Wang Libo, Gao Yinying, Zhang Jiantao
Mechanical engineering team: Liu Hai, He Meng, Li Chaoying, Xiang Bo, Zhen Yi
Gross floor area: 5,700 square meters
Completion: 2015
Photography: Zhang Guangyuan

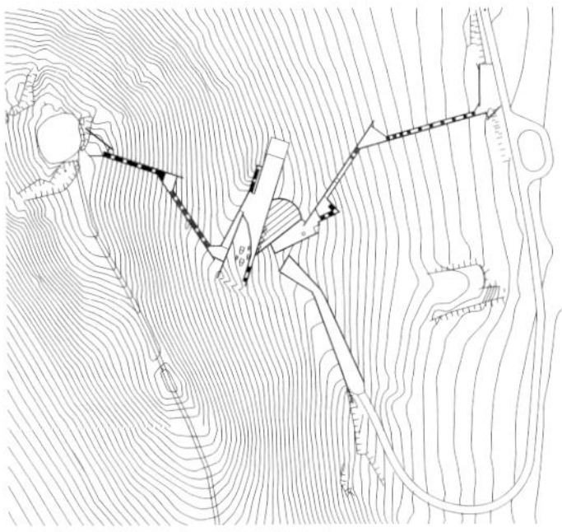

Site plan

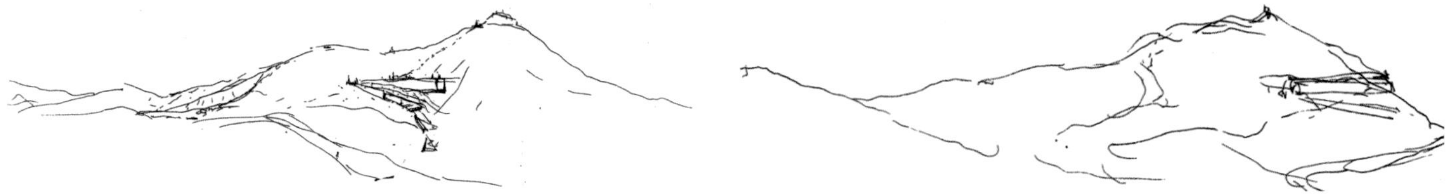

Sketch of the museum in context

The Site of Xanadu Museum is a supporting attraction to the Site of Xanadu UNESCO World Heritage attraction. Its main functions include the exhibition of cultural relics, providing public services for the Xanadu attraction sites, and as an archive repository; it also has offices and spaces for archaeological studies.

The museum is located on the eastern Xanadu-facing side of the Wulantai Mountain, about 5 kilometers to the south of the site itself. Visitors arrive from the south and walk around the foot of the hill, unable to see the museum entrance until it suddenly reveals itself. The main part of the museum utilizes an abandoned quarry, revamping the mountain damaged by mining activities. The staff entrance is located at the southern end of an existing zigzagging mining trench, while offices and archaeological research facilities are located at the sides of the trench under a soil cover in line with the mountain's profile. A circular mining hole is remodeled as a sunken courtyard for the museum with public service areas surrounding it.

Based on the principle of minimizing interferences with the heritage site, only an elongated cuboidal viewing deck of the museum is exposed, while most of the museum's architecture is buried and hidden within the mountain. This design stands as a metaphor for the buried ruins of the Site of Xanadu. This viewing deck itself is rotated eastward at 18 degrees from true north and intersects the mountain's contour lines. It points directly to the location of the former Mingde Gate, which stands on the central axis of the Site of Xanadu. It links the architecture of the museum with the relics in terms of a perfect visual angle and axial connection. From the perspective of the Mingde Gate, the view of the museum shrinks into a tiny square, emphasizing the respect for the environmental integrity of the site and the harmonious dialogue between humankind and nature.

A series of platforms overlooking the Site of Xanadu and the surrounding grassland is set along the indoor and outdoor visitor routes of the museum that end at an *ovoo*, a sacred Mongolian stone altar on the top of the mountain. The path and the platforms are inseparable parts of the museum, which connect the history, culture, and landscapes of Xanadu.

In order to reflect the name Wulantai Mountain, which means "beacon on the red rocks" in Mongolian, the exterior wall of the architecture, the platforms, and the retaining wall are made of bare concrete mixed with iron oxide, giving the exposed architecture a mottled red color. This results in the museum becoming an extension of the mountain itself, which stays in harmony with the seasonal changes in the hilly grassland, presenting a kind of spatial quality of vast desolation.

Distant view from the east

Since its completion, the project has won numerous awards, including the 2019 ARCASIA Award for Architecture. The jury gave the following remarks on the project:

"Built five kilometers across a Mongolian grassland from the Xanadu archaeological site known locally as Wulantai, meaning 'beacon on the red rocks,' this museum is a beacon of great architecture in its own right. Mostly embedded in the pit formed from an abandoned quarry, it emerges from the earth in a geometric collection of iron oxide-infused concrete. The structure's unpredictable angularity and the protruding windows are a remark on a history that is often nonlinear. Oriented to intersect with both the mountain's contours and the starting point of the capital city ruin's central axis, it positions people within a territorial dialogue between the artificial and the natural, if not the terrestrial and the celestial."

Main entrance hidden inside

View of the rooftop

Outdoor staircase

Sunken courtyard

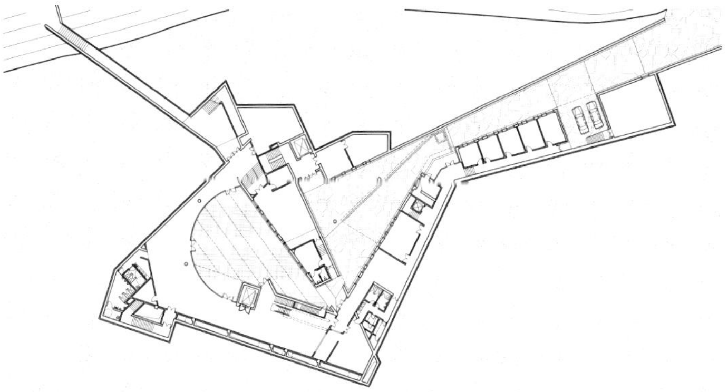

Basement floor plan

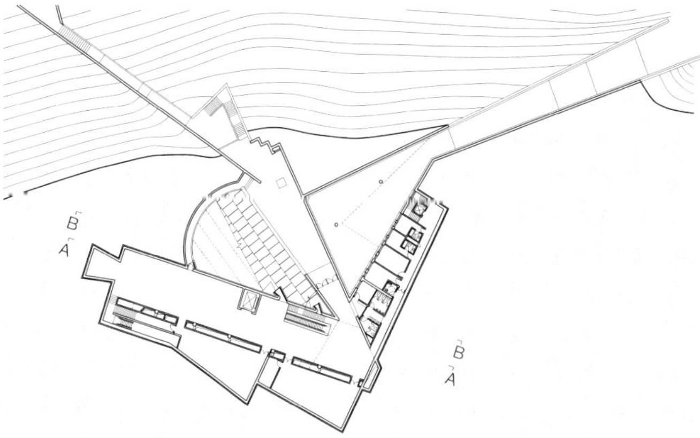

Ground-floor plan

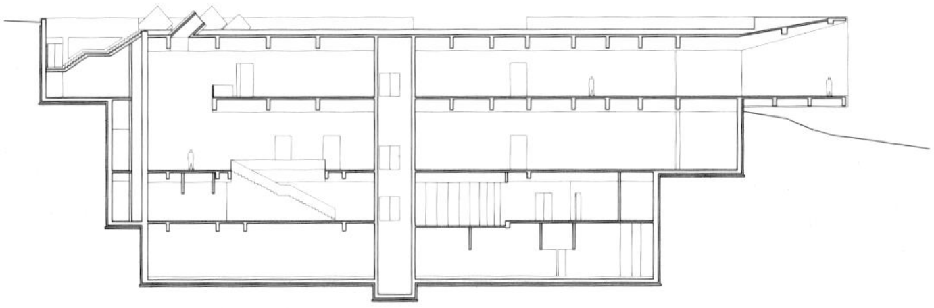

Section A-A

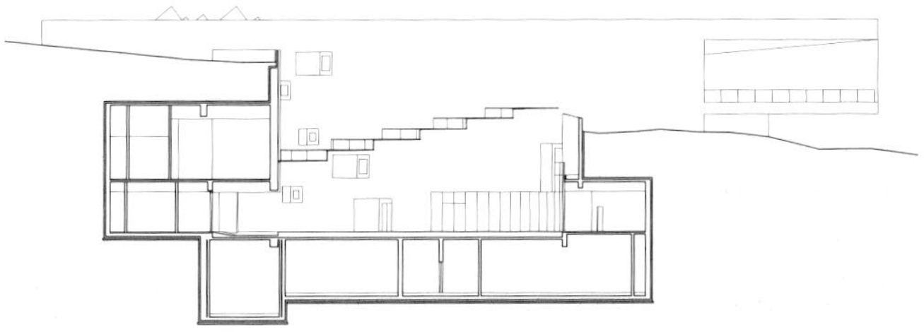

Section B-B

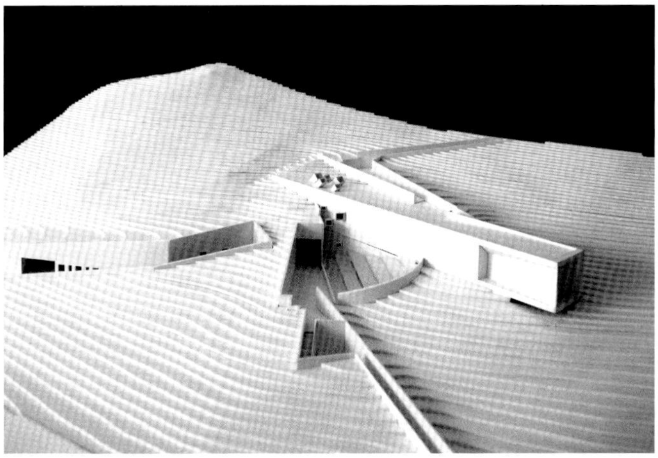

Model

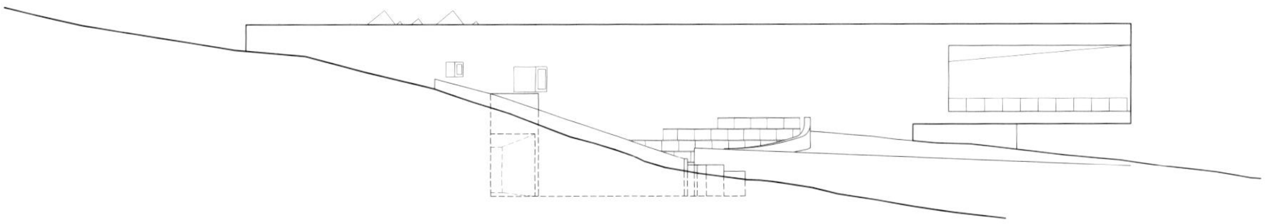

Elevation

JIXI MUSEUM

Location: Jixi, Anhui Province, China
Architect: Atelier Li Xinggang
Principal architect: Li Xinggang
Design team: Zhang Yinxuan, Zhang Zhe, Xing Di, Zhang Yiting, Yi Lingjie, Zhong Manlin
Structure design team: Wang Libo, Yang Wei, Liang Wei
Mechanical engineering team: He Meng, Li Jingsha, Zhang Qian, Li Junmin, Ding Zhiqiang
Landscape design team: Li Li, Yu Chao
Gross floor area: 10,000 square meters
Completion: 2013
Photography: Xia Zhi, Li Xinggang, Li Zhe

Site plan

Aerial view

The Jixi Museum is located in the northern part of the old town of Jixi County in the eastern Chinese province of Anhui. Historically, the site was the location of the county government and the town hall. As part of a comprehensive preservation and restoration project of the entire old town, the site has been repurposed to create a comprehensive museum on local culture and history that will feature exhibition spaces, a 4D cinema, a range of guest relations services, shops, offices and administration, and storage facilities.

The design is based on surveys of the landscape, the origin of the name Jixi, as well as investigations into the local traditional Hui-style settlements. The entire building is covered by a continuous roof with an undulating profile, in a texture that mimics the mountains and rivers surrounding the county. It is the logical result and expression of the shape of Jixi. Once the other buildings in the old town are restored to the Hui-style design, the museum will fit in more naturally with the entire town.

In order to preserve as many of the existing trees on the site as possible, multiple courtyards, patios, and lanes were introduced into the overall layout of the complex. At the same time, the design reinterprets the spatial layout of the vernacular Hui architecture while creating comfortable outdoor spaces. Two streams run along the lanes, one on the east, and the other on the west of the building cluster, finally converging into a pool in the large courtyard at the main entrance. In the south part of the building is a *mingtang*, a typical interior courtyard often seen in the layout of Huizhou-style houses, which follows the traditional Chinese principles of feng shui. Directly opposite the main entrance is an abstract formation of rocks. A visitor's route leads past the *mingtang* to a viewing platform in the southeast corner of the building, where visitors are presented with a bird's-eye view of the roofscape, courtyards, and the distant mountains.

With a sloping degree adapted from local buildings, the triangular structural steel trusses function well with the undulating roof. Local building materials such as bricks and clay tiles are used in modern and innovative ways to pay respect to history, while responding to the present.

Main courtyard and Ming Hall

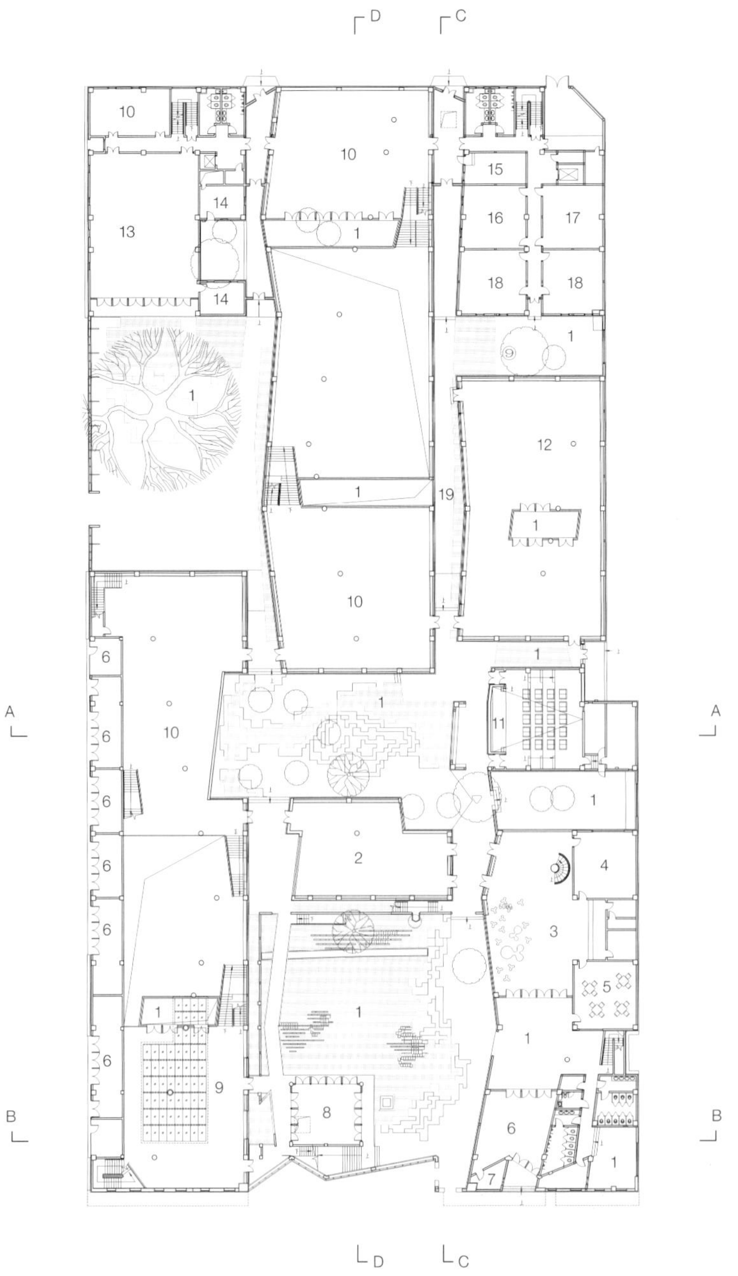

Ground-floor plan

1. Patio
2. Preface hall
3. Reception hall
4. VIP room
5. Classroom
6. Shop
7. Ticket booth
8. Tea pavilion
9. Reserved relic site
10. Exhibition hall
11. 4D-cinema
12. Temporary exhibition hall
13. Lecture hall
14. Equipment
15. Fire control room
16. Technology and management room
17. Temporary storage
18. Storage facilities
19. Lane

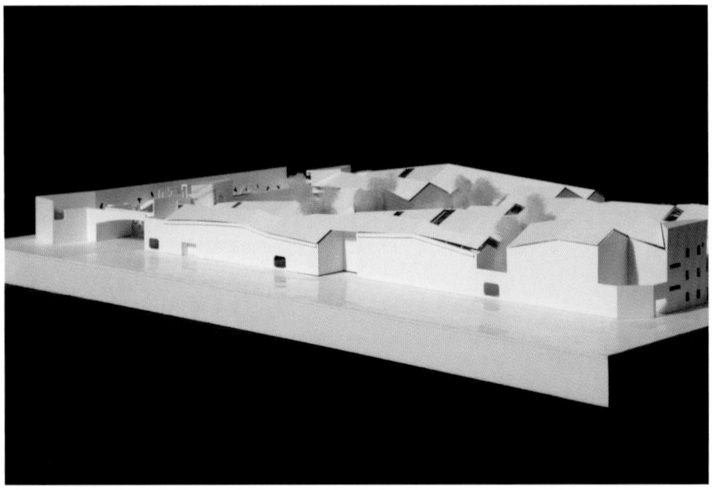

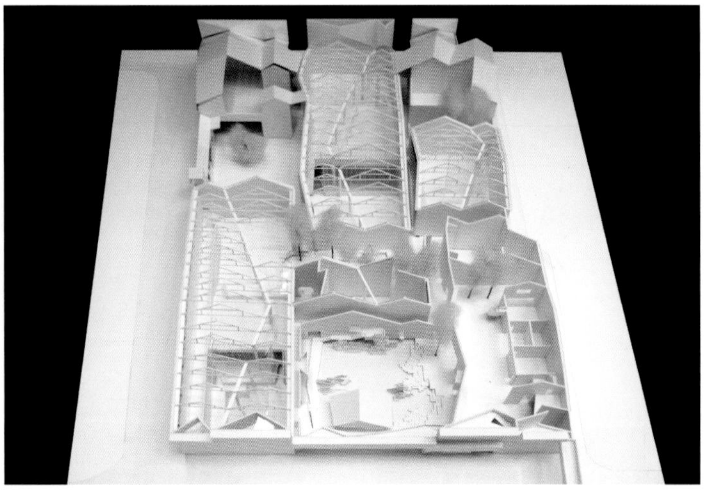

Model

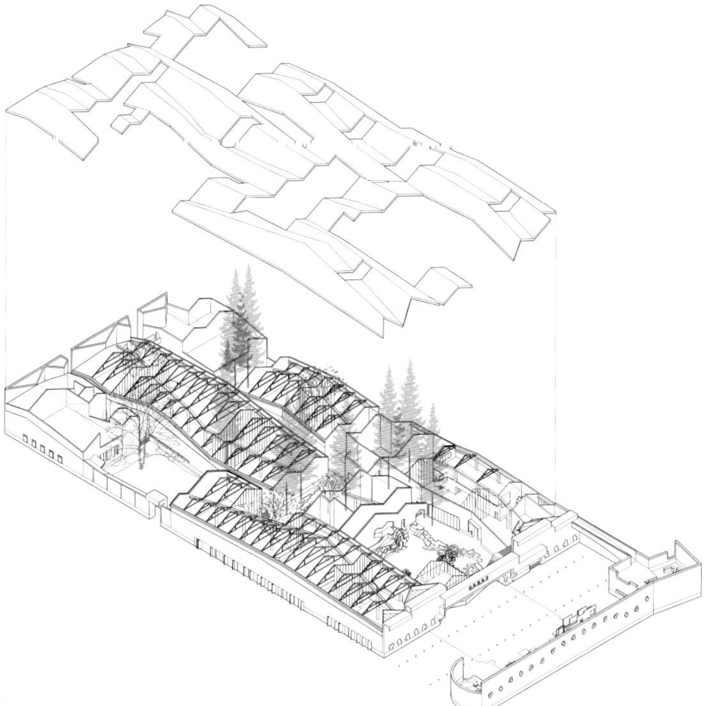

Axonometric drawing

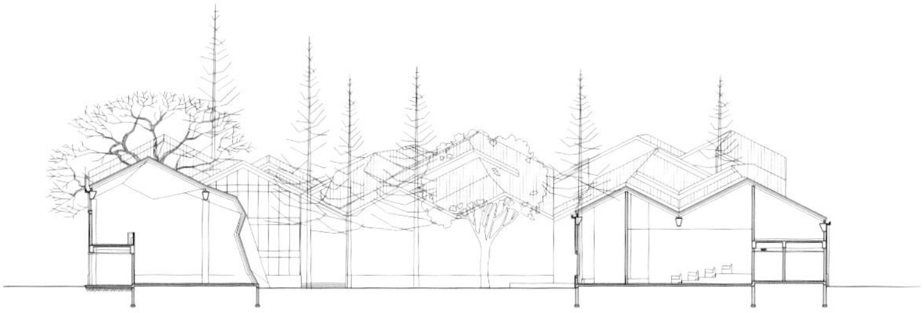

Section A-A

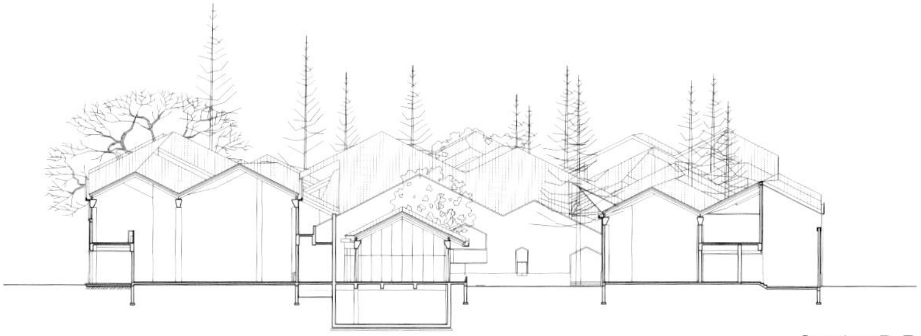

Section B-B

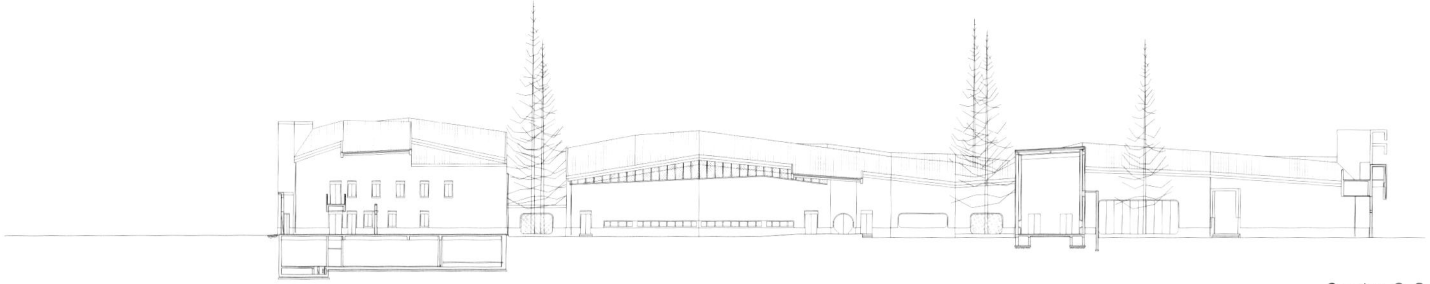

Section C-C

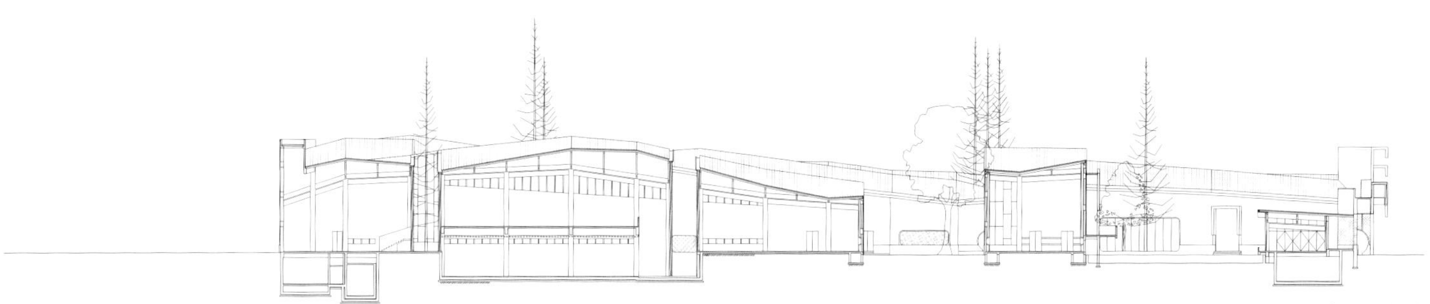

Section D-D

Philip F. Yuan

Archi-Union Architects
Professor at the College of Architecture and Urban Planning (CAUP), Tongji University
Director of the Digital Design Research Center (DDRC)
Founding partner of Archi-Union Architects and Fab-Union Technology

Founded in 2003 in Shanghai, Archi-Union has always focused on the ontological research of construction with a critical vision. Through the cutting-edge exploration of the design laboratory, it aims to break the binary opposition between research and practice, open up ideological boundaries, and expand the openness of architecture and its possibilities, thus advancing both research and practice.

Based on a new construction perspective of building materials, new contemporary connotations are endowed upon digital and intelligent means of architecture for the international avant-garde. Committed to the effective integration of architectural design theory, technology, local cultures, and the zeitgeist, Archi-Union specifically focuses on the application of digital design and intelligent construction methods to practical construction projects.

Archi-Union has been invited to participate in exhibitions around the world, including the 2019 Bi-City Biennale of Urbanism/Architecture, the 2018 Venice Biennale of Architecture, a 2018 solo exhibition at Architektur Galerie Berlin and the Fab-Union Space Shanghai, the 2017 Shanghai Urban Space Art Season, and the 2017 Chicago Architecture Biennial, among others. Additionally, the Museum of Modern Art has acquired models and pedestals from Archi-Union's In Bamboo and Pond Society projects as permanent collections.

Selected Works

2011 Tea House, Shanghai, China
2011 Silk Wall & J office, Shanghai, China
2012 Design of Beichuan Earthquake Memorial Mall, Sichuan, China
2014 Dacheng Vertical Park, Shenzhen, China
2015 Fab-Union Space, Shanghai, China
2015 Songjiang Art Campus, Shanghai, China
2015 Novartis Campus Office building C11-1 Office, Shanghai, China
2016 Jade Museum, Shanghai, China
2016 Chi She, Shanghai, China
2016 Ceramic House, Shanghai, China
2017 International School (Sanhao Middle School Renovation), Shanghai, China
2017 Suzhou Garden Expo Main Hall, Suzhou, China
2017 Sinan Bookstore, Shanghai, China
2017 In Bamboo, Daoming, China
2017 Cloud Village, Chongzhou, China
2017 Cloud Pavilion at the Dripping Lake, Shanghai, China
2018 Daoming Bamboo Craft Village, Sichuan, China
2018 Cyborg Fabrication – Venue B of Shanghai Westbund World Artificial Intelligence Conference, Shanghai, China
2019 ShanghART Gallery West Bund Space Renovation & Renewal Design, Shanghai, China
2019 Light of Internet World Internet Conference Center, Wuzhen, China
2019 Inkstone House OCT Linpan Cultural Center, Anren, China
2019 Yongan Warehouse, Shanghai, China
2019 Organic embedded, HengMian cement plant reconstruction, Shanghai, China

Interviewer: Fang Ziyu
Interviewee: Philip F. Yuan (Yuan)
Editor: Mo Wanli

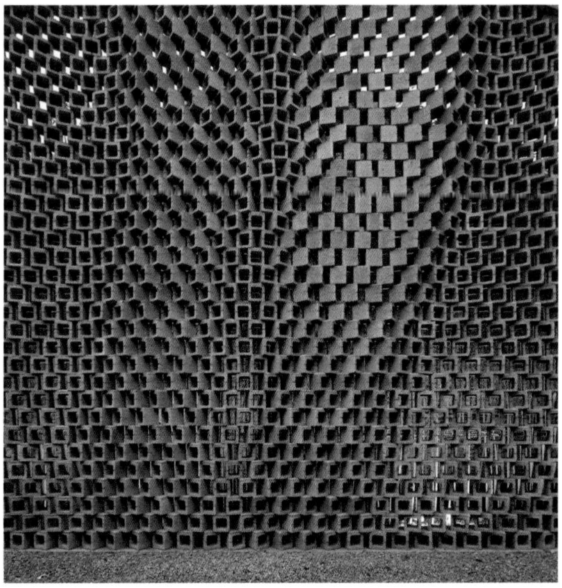

Silk Wall © Shen Zhonghai

What is your understanding of "building with nature?"

YUAN: Taking a literal view of "building with nature," most people will probably interpret it through the lens of "the age of humanity." They'll use humankind as the subject for viewing the relationship between human beings and nature. This includes the way architecture integrates with the natural environment or the locality of materials. But I want to rethink "building with nature" from the context of the post-human era. Within that context, objects are seen as capable of possessing intelligence and information, which means that nature itself—or the ecosphere—has subjectivity. This is the advent of the era of hyperobjects. "Building with nature" will not simply emphasize locality or building with local materials, but point toward a pan-natural hierarchy. It shall create a new understanding of the term itself and its meaning from the integrated perspectives of existing ecospheres, globalization, technological iteration, and new knowledge communities. The emergence of COVID-19 should prompt us to clearly consider this: humankind should no longer be the sole subject within the narrow meaning of existence, nor should we simply focus on humanism. Instead, we need to re-examine the equality between humans, objects, and nature, with all three enjoying the same rights and benefits. As technology develops and the human capacity to transform the earth continues to grow, we need to respect our living environment and the laws of its ecosystem even more, and we need to find a sustainable way of surviving in this new equilibrium.

In the past, craftspeople used to physically practice construction, so our understanding of construction aesthetics relates to the human scale and experience, from which Le Corbusier's Modulor Man arose. But the contemporary construction arising from human–machine collaboration already moved well beyond the scale of the human body. This development has disrupted the interfaces that humans can operate and the human experience in general, as well as enabled more construction choices. As a result, the aesthetic meaning of architecture no longer only serves manmade aesthetics. Therefore, the significance of architecture lies not only in its service to human aesthetics, but also in the creation of a new ethical aesthetic form which enables the harmonious coexistence between humans and the earth. From this standpoint, I believe that architecture as a discipline needs a new, systematic, philosophical approach, and has the responsibility to examine predictions of the future.

What sorts of opportunities led you to explore this direction?

YUAN: I spent six years working at Joint Studio at MIT, from 2003 to 2009. I received broad support from the former chair, Stanford Anderson, and his successor, Yung Ho Chang, so I officially started moving toward my current research direction in 2009. Beginning in 2011, I worked with Professor Neil Leach to create a series of activities called DigitalFUTURES, which was supported by Qingyun Ma, the then dean of the University of South California (USC). As it were, the earliest initiators of this platform were Tongji University and USC; after 2013, support came from Tongji University and companies like the Tongji Architectural Design (Group) and Trendzone. Neil Leach and I recognized early on, the potential technological and philosophical impact of technology on the field of architecture. We saw that the emerging knowledge systems would be more than merely tools, being more new epistemological and methodological starting points. From there, we tried to turn the DigitalFUTURES program into a new knowledge community platform centered around a global mindset. With over eighty workshops, thirty speeches, and more than 10,000 registered participants across the world today, we are far larger than any university. DigitalFUTURES was recently awarded the 2020 ACADIA Academic Program Award of Excellence, a recognition from the global knowledge community to the contributions that DigitalFUTURES has made to education.

How does this direction of exploration relate to your practice?

YUAN: In recent years, I have led the studio to verify the feasibility of the new tools and new methods we're exploring in architectural practices, like our platform for robotic construction and digital factory. We want to see if it's possible to use a small workforce to produce high-performance, high-quality construction, along with leaner details and finishes. It's an attempt to discuss the division of labor in, and the upgrade of the construction industry. Although the many results of the explorations into the building process have not yet been released, overall, the actual progress will be better than what we have seen so far. I'm confident that we will gradually see more experimental projects and that they will have a profound impact on the development of the construction industry in the near future.

FAB-UNION SPACE

Location: Building D, Longtengdadao, Xuhui District, Shanghai, China
Architect: Archi-Union Architects
Principal architect: Philip F. Yuan
Design team: Alex Han, Kong Xiangping, Wang Xuwei
Structure design team: Zhang Zhun
Gross floor area: 368 square meters
Completion: 2015
Photography: Chen Hao, Su Shengliang

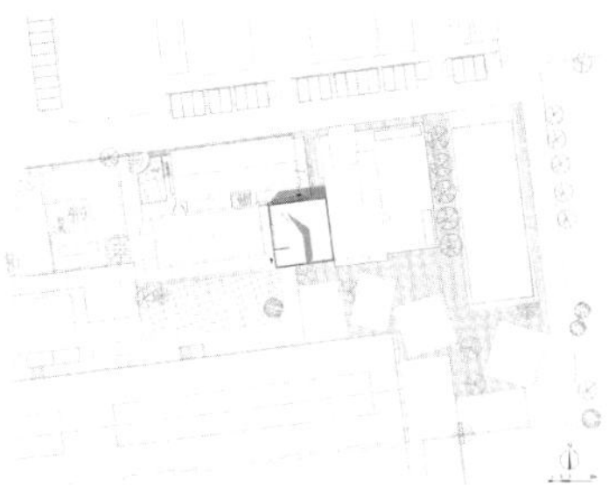

Site plan

Entrance to the Fab-Union Space

Within the process of rapid urbanization, the creation of micro-buildings often requires the highly efficient use of land, and the formation of universal spaces, while creating a unique spatial character and charm for the city and the building itself.

The Fab-Union Space, located in Shanghai's West Bund culture and arts district, is a small-sized building with about 300 square meters of floor area. At the beginning of the design process, in order to reduce the amount of investment and improve its spatial efficiency, the entire project was divided horizontally into two elongated spaces. The floors on each side of the divide feature different elevations to maximize the usable area while providing sufficient flexibility for potential future uses, such as exhibitions and offices. Both floors are supported on the outside by two 150-millimeter-thick concrete walls. In the center, gravity is guided downward by the clever layout of a vertical staircase. This center thus supports the entire building, assimilating the traditionally dualistic architectural elements of structure and passage space.

Simultaneously, the main passage and its gravitational requirements limit each other to find a balance, naturally forming the basis for the spatial shape. The building's interface is left relatively transparent, so that the structure's expressive power can be seen from outside.

The design concept had to ensure that the double-height exhibition hall on both sides and the third-floor single-story exhibition hall, once completed, left only 3 meters of space for the passage in the center. This space is conceptualized to frame the dynamic behavior of people, allow airflow, and mazimize the continuity of the design's spatial volume.

In turn, the nonlinear creation of this space is based on the optimization of its structural performance and spatial dynamics. The entire process uses a variety of design methods including stone cutting, projective geometry, and algorithmic shaping.

As a plastic material, concrete creates an expressive structure while still making the space feel otherworldly. The completion of the entire project took only four months from design to construction, which can be considered a miracle made possible by digital design and construction methods.

Exhibition *Steven Holl: Making Architecture*

Exhibition space

Wrapped concrete structure

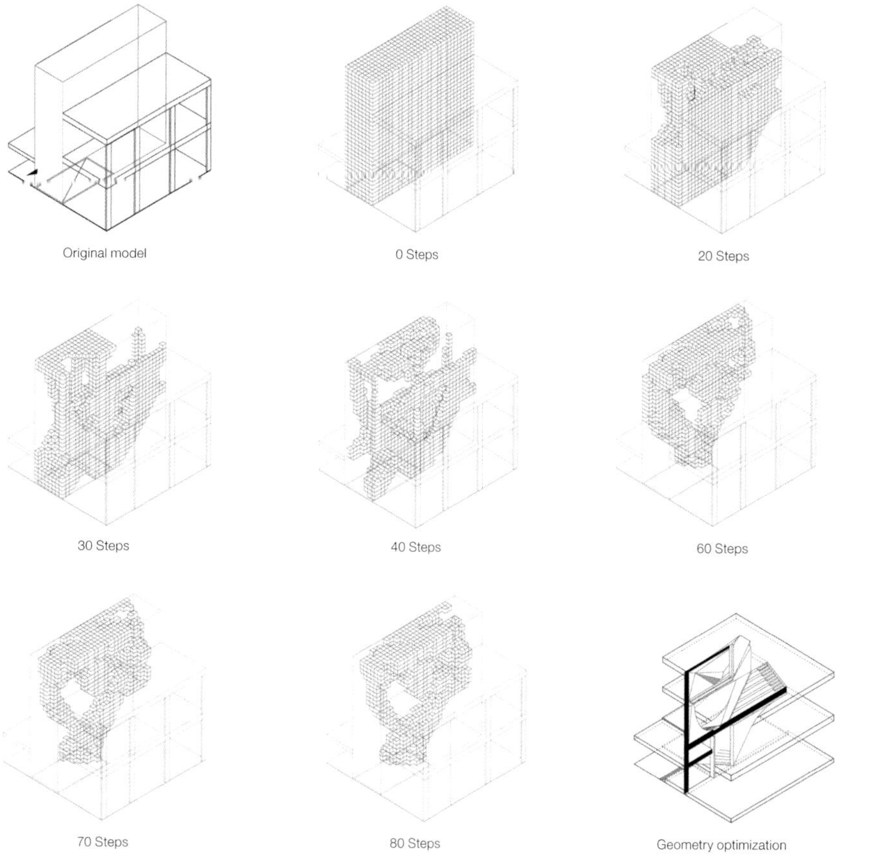

Evolutionary structure optimization diagram

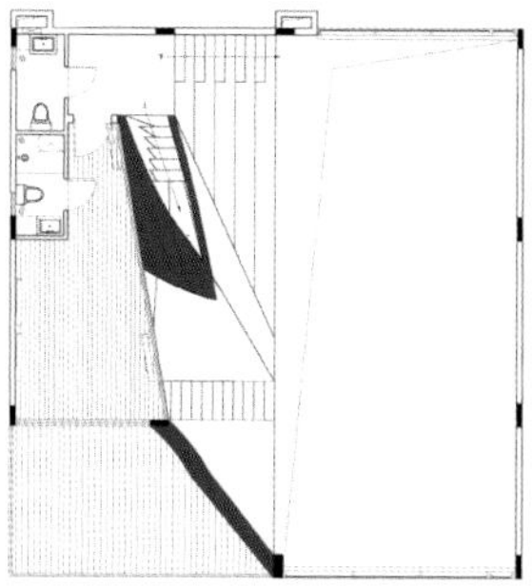

6.93-meter-floor plan

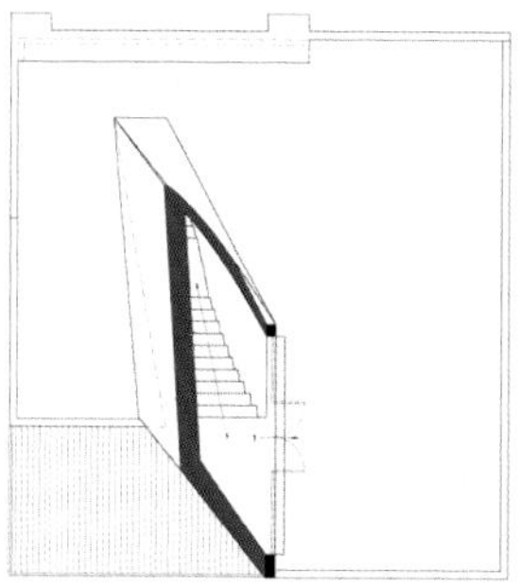

Rooftop floor plan

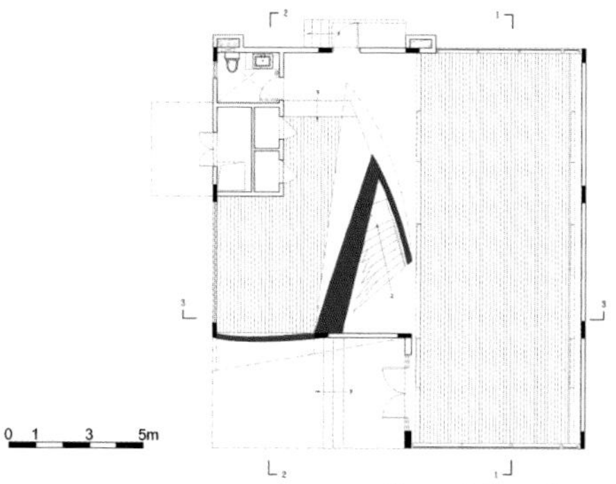

Ground-floor plan

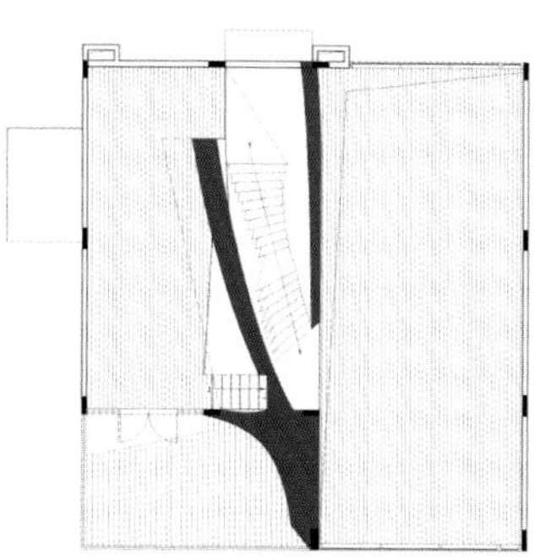

3.4-meter-floor plan

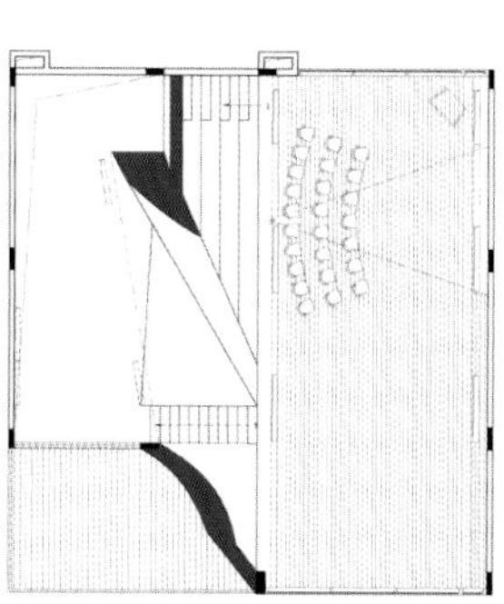

Second-floor plan

CHI SHE

Location: Building D, No. 2555 Longtengdadao, Xuhui District, Shanghai, China
Architect: Archi-Union Architects
Principal architect: Philip F. Yuan
Design team: Alex Han, Xiangping Kong, Tianrui Zhu, Qinrong Liu
Structure design team: Rui Wang, Junchao Shen, Xiaofeng Zhang, Jin Wang
Interior design team: Xuwei Wang, Xiaoming Chen
Mechanical design team: Yong Liu, Changying Jiang, Xi Li
Digital fabrication: Fab-Union Intelligent Engineering Co. Ltd.
Gross floor area: 199 square meters
Design period: February 2016–March 2016
Construction period: April 2019–September 2016
Photography: Philip F. Yuan, Su Shengliang

Site plan

Chi She is the name of a group of artists founded by Zhang Peili and Geng Jiangyi, characterized by their interest in realism. Their exhibition space in the West Bund Art Exhibition Area seeks to evoke an enigmatic spatial appeal through the harmonizing and integration of the building with its surroundings, while at the same time offering a formal expression of the artistic mission of the works contained inside. The hope is that this building might provide a sensitive and generous art space where various artistic events, such as exhibitions, creative workshops, and informal communication can occur.

The existing exterior walls were retained, shored up and structurally reinforced as needed, in order to achieve the maximum space possible. In order not to affect the space perception of this area, part of Chi She's roof has been lifted up to give those inside an unobstructed view of the sky. The roofing structure has been replaced by a more efficient, lightweight, tensioned timber structure, a section of which has been raised to bring in the light and connect those inside to the changing climate outside. Gray-green bricks were chosen to blend in with the existing structure and are applied to the exterior surface to offer an interface with the coutryard. The entrance wall has been warped slightly, as a form of architectural expression that conveys current cultural trends based on tradition.

In order to complete such a complex form of masonry construction that could not have been achieved using traditional methods, robotic masonry fabrication techniques were employed on-site, utilizing advanced digital fabrication technology. The external walls were built using recycled gray-green bricks salvaged from the old building and constructed with the help of a technologically advanced robotic arm to generate a curved surface that expresses the vitality of the Chi community.

The precise positioning of the masonry using robotic fabrication technologies transforms the traditional materials of bricks and mortar and allows them to be seen in a new era and in a new light. The integration of these salvaged bricks into a new stretch of curving wall narrates a story of people and bricks, machines and construction, and design and culture, which will be etched into the shadows of the external wall under the setting sun.

"Waving" façade

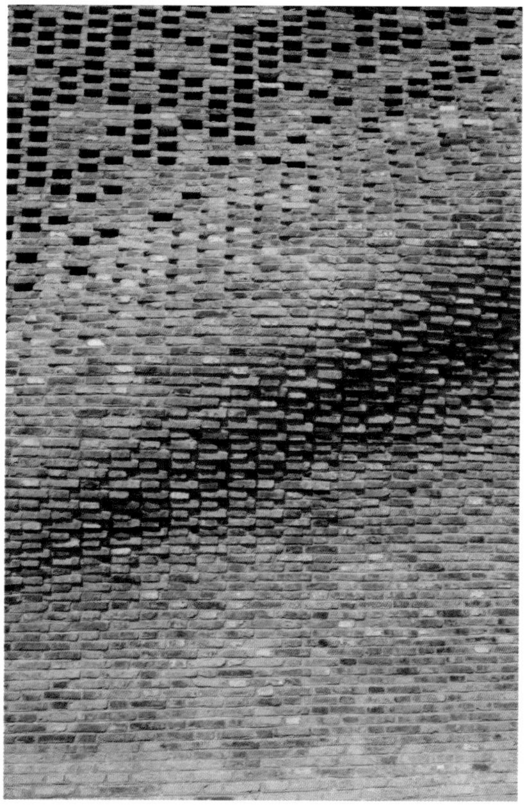

Façade details

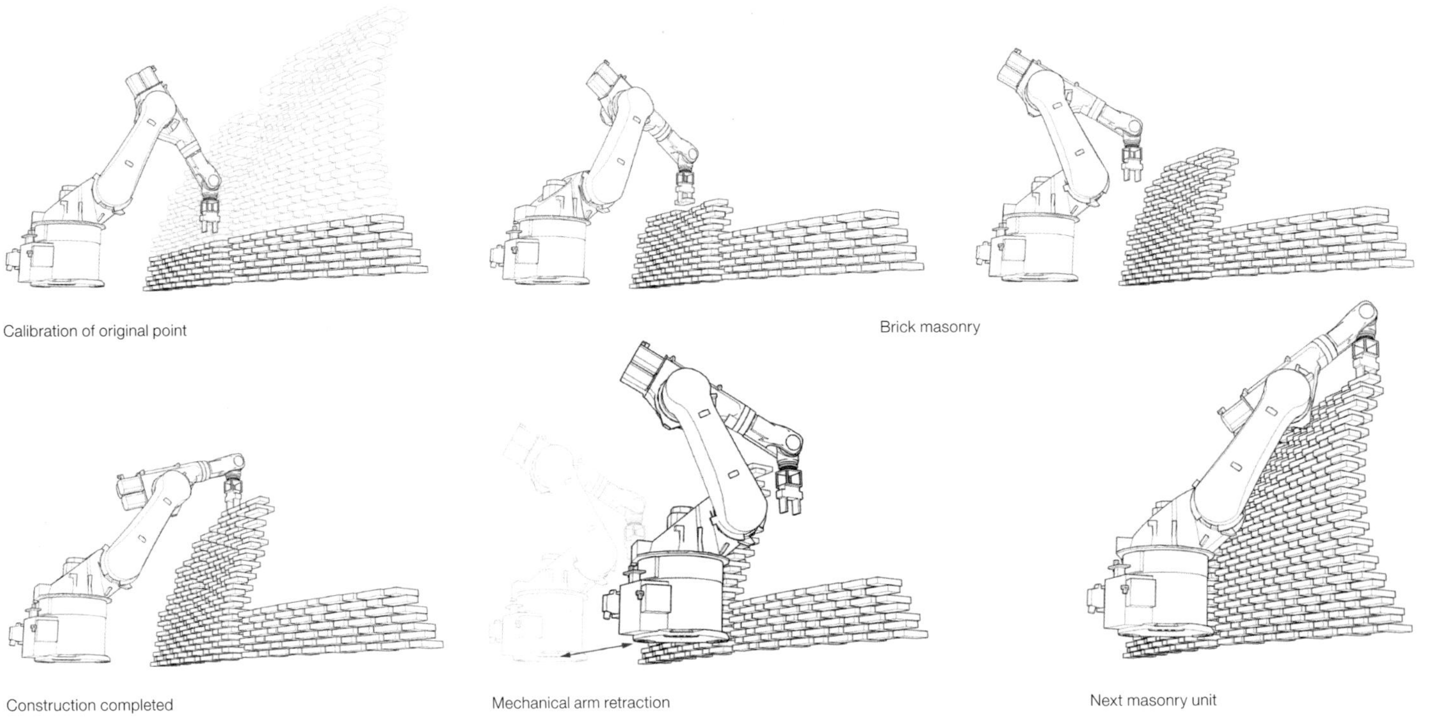

Construction process diagram

Close-up of robotic construction

Robotic construction

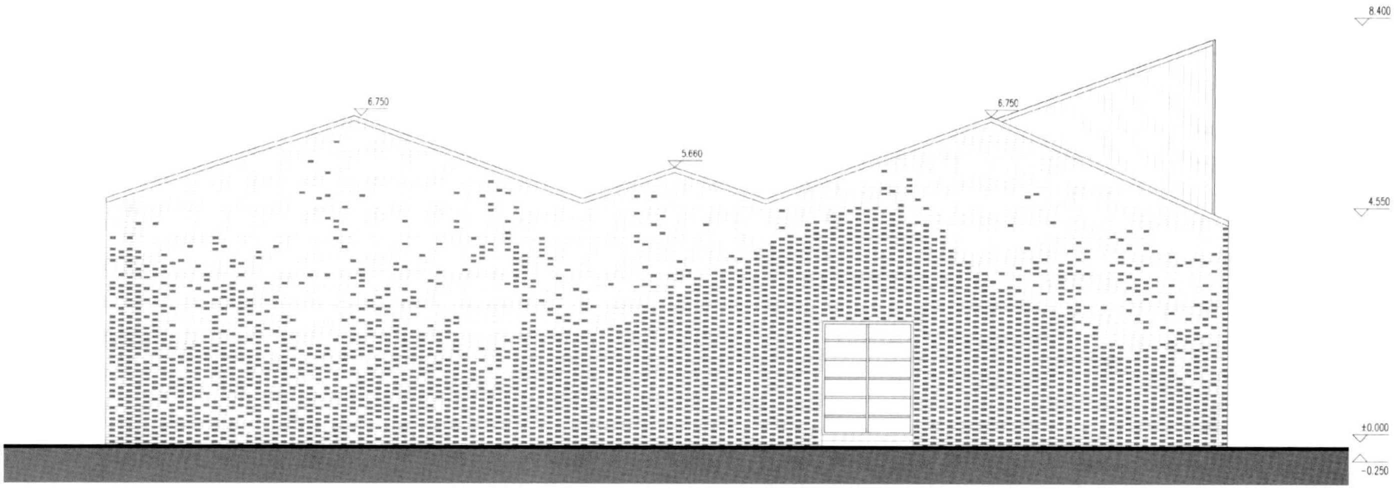

East elevation

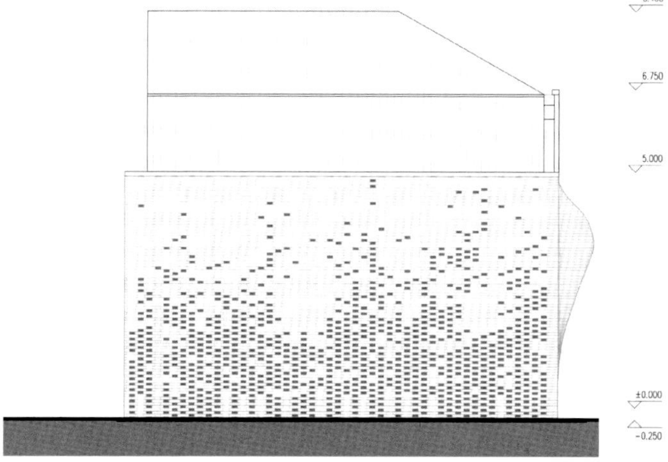

South elevation

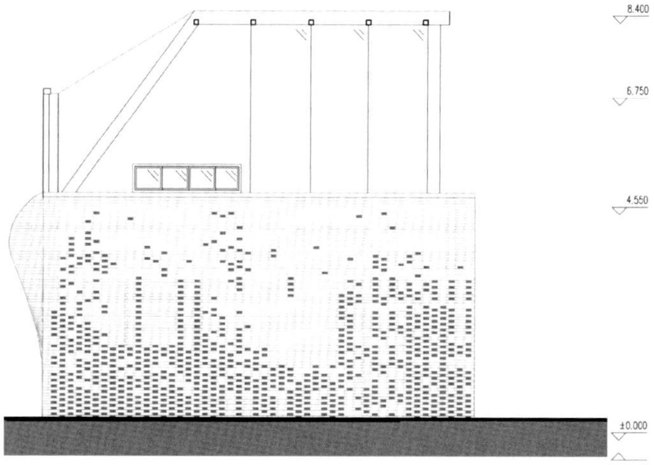

North elevation

自然建造
ARCHITECTURE
CHINA
AWARD

EXPLORATION AWARD FOR YOUNG ARCHITECTS

The Exploration Award for Young Architects will be granted to young architects under the age of forty-five with two or more high-quality works completed in recent years. It aims to show professional recognition while encouraging the experimental spirit of young architects.

Wang Hao
Untitled Architects

Laureate

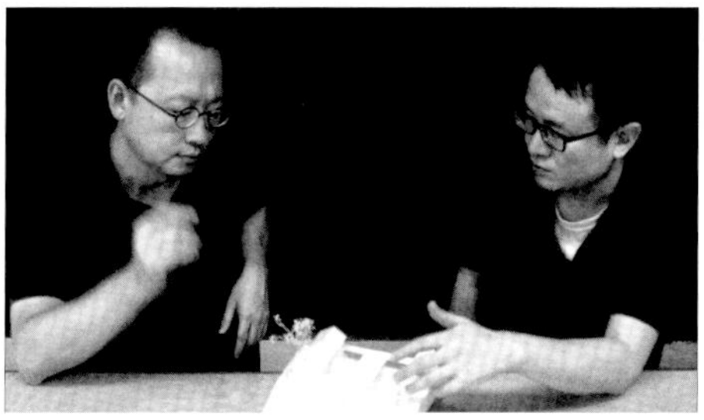

Liu Kenan + Zhang Xu
Atelier XÜK

Laureate

Liu Chang + Gao Qin + Kong Dezhong
Atelier Sounding Architecture

Laureate

Shui Yanfei + Su Yichi
NATURALBUILD

Shortlisted

Wang Baozhen
Yinyuan Studio

Shortlisted

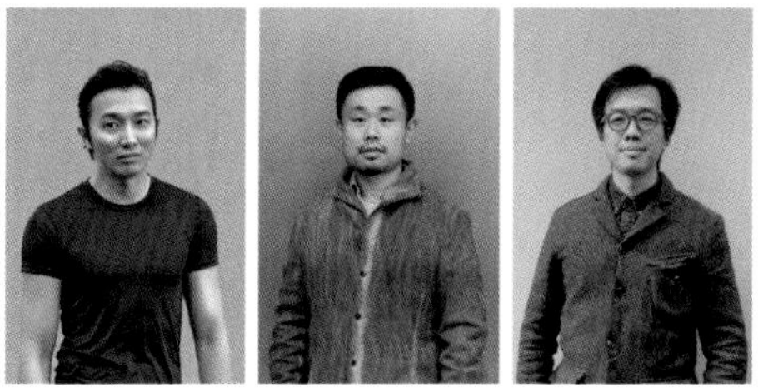

Huang Zhe + Huang Li + Zhang Yao
OfficeOffCourse

Shortlisted

Wang Hao

Untitled Architects

The practice of Untitled Architects is dedicated to discovering the uniqueness of the vernacular region. Facing different scales of villages, towns and cities, Untitled Architects explores the social order and logic of spatial extension in the contemporary context, and carries out urban design and architectural practices such as improving traditional crafts, awakening the language of materials, and reshaping structural systems.

Wang Hao's practice and research are focused on local crafts and construction in the towns and the countryside of southern China. He was awarded the BAUWELT Prize for First Works in 2015. His works have been exhibited in *"Free Structure: New Chinese Habitat" Solo Exhibition* (Shanghai Design Center, 2013), *2015 Shanghai Urban Space Art Season*, and at The Chinese Pavilion at the 15th Venice Biennale (2016). Since 2015, he has also been teaching at the School of Architecture at the China Academy of Art as a visiting professor. He is also the founder of the Construction Society Jian Zao Xue She, which is an academic group focused on the research of Chinese wooden residential architecture and crafts.

Selected Works

2009 Ku House in Chunxiao, Ningbo, China
2011 Wang House in Chunxiao, Ningbo, China
2013 Ke House in Chunxiao, Ningbo, China
2014 Keli Museum, Ningbo, China
2015 Cixi House No. 5, Ningbo, China
2016 Shanghai House No. 2, Shanghai, China
2017 Rùn Inn, Ninghai, China
2018 Luobei Guiyuan New Village Renovation, Shaoxing, China
2018 Qiantong Culture Center, Ninghai, China
2018 Beilun Warehouse (under construction), Ningbo, China
2019 Xiaoyue Pavilion, Shaoxing, China
2019 Suichang People's Hospital (under construction), Lishui, China
2019 Ci Town Feng Jicai Library (under construction), Ningbo, China

1. Qiantong Culture Center © Chen Hao
2. Qiantong Culture Center interior © Chen Hao

Interviewer: Fang Ziyu
Interviewee: Wang Hao (Wang)
Editor: Mo Wanli

What is your understanding of "building with nature?"

WANG: Nature is the mother of all things. The materials that people have used to transform nature over millennia have evolved from basic wood and stone to concrete, glass, plastic, and other artificial materials. The way materials are organized have also evolved: from manual laying or weaving by individual workers to large-scale machine prefabrication and on-site mechanical support. Above the organization of materials lies the organization of groups of buildings. My understanding of "building with nature" is a partial return to the way primitive materials and primitive building groups were organized. These architectural spaces, like the majority of pre-modern villages, move closer to the essence of human life. The organization of these spatial groups and building materials can be traced to the natural environment—permeable and capable of poeticism. To me, "building" and "nature" represent two laws. Nature guides the organization of the "groups," while building represents the "weaving" of materials.

This understanding emerges within a context that fully mobilizes the efficiency of the contemporary builder. Nature is hard to tame; working with nature requires that we grasp its laws. One of those ways might be to follow a hybrid approach: a mix of traditional and modern-day craftsmanship, a collage of modern-day design and traditional genetics.

Shanghai House No. 2 © Chen Hao

What are the main directions that your practice is currently exploring?

WANG: One direction is "hollow structures," the key word being "channels." I am developing a series of wind, light and water channels—channels meant to shoulder the responsibility of opening up sealed and formatted bodies—for example, turning an array of columns into a 10-kilometer-long pine forest, and transforming it into a graceful natural system beyond simple modules and abstractions. I tried this recently in the Suichang Mortuary and the Suichang People's Hospital projects. Another major direction is timber constructions; Rùn Inn is the first project to fully demonstrate my thinking and outlook on this.

Looking back at it today, this overarching direction started in 2010 with a deep dive into the theme at the time: "free structures." My personal conclusion revolves around structurally arranging objects of nature (like wind, light, and water), weaving them into the construction, and manifesting them into the material system. To this end, I've experimented with red bricks, gray bricks, steel, fair-faced concrete, and even solid wood. Prior to 2015, I primarily explored possibilities with concrete and steel in private residence projects. In 2015, I began teaching at the Chinese Academy of Art and started looking more closely at the wood element. My studies turned traditional timber structures on their heads mechanically and explored the way they can feed into modern-day designs. Experimenting with improvements to timber construction is a long-term plan, and has been in the process five years now. Despite that, we are still pursuing this from the perspective of an open, research-driven practice.

Wang House © Untitled Architects

Keli Museum in Ningbo © Liu Xiaoguang

Luobei Guiyuan New Village Renovation © Chen Hao

What are the greatest challenges and opportunities facing young architects today?

WANG: Creating good living spaces as a way of providing for the society remains a challenge for architects today. According to curator Cui Cancan, vulnerability and romance are the only dignities in this age of mediocrity. Young architects like us are small fry when it comes to the housing sector, whether it's private or public housing. We have no way of creating a space with the slightest shred of romance for the public. Our society has a severe shortage of good, affordable, romantic spaces, which is a problem that architects have to solve. Architects truly need to possess sensitivity and a long antenna; they need to excel at discovering where they're needed.

These are the opportunities. The challenges still lie in whether or not architects can guide communities, save abandoned villages, advocate for the toilet revolution, pass on traditional construction methods, raise design-assistance funds, pioneer the renovations of rural residences, and safeguard urban villages.

GUIYUAN NEW VILLAGE RENOVATION

Location: Shaoxing, Zhejiang Province, China
Architect: Untitled Architects
Principal architect: Wang Hao
Design team: Chen Siyu
Gross floor area: 1,200 square meters
Design period: March 2017–May 2017
Construction period: June 2017–January 2018
Photography: Chen Hao, Guo Guozhu

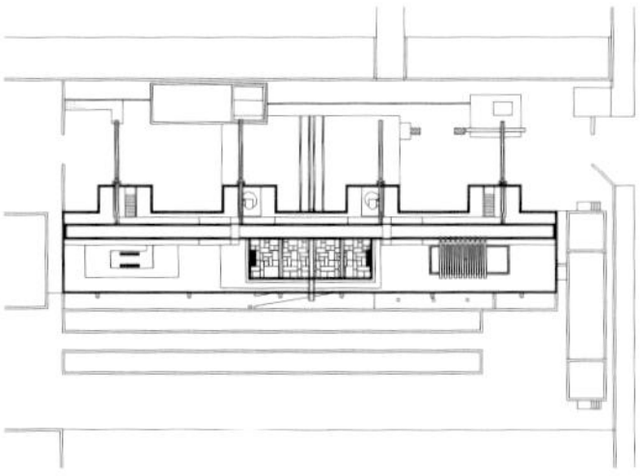

Site plan

Aerial view

The No. 32 Guiyuan New Village site was historically the staff quarters for a state-owned textile company in Shaoxing. Built in the 1980s, Guiyuan resembles other newly built villages typical of that time, except that there are one or two concrete flat houses sitting between the residential buildings. The flat houses are about 50 meters long and 2 meters wide. Independent doors made from a range of materials can be seen from the exterior, creating a linear space with an unfinished two-story building between them. The building is composed of four residential units, each hosting a standard 60-square-meter floor space, including two bedrooms and one living room. The kitchen, bathroom, and living room are located on the north side while the two bedrooms are on the south side.

Deduction 1. Peeling off the plaster to expose the wall bricks: while looking for clues to guide the spatial design, I noticed the long corridor in the south. It inspired me to open up the spaces on the north side in order to create a new gallery space. The plaster coating of the original concrete masonry structure was removed to pay respect to the original red brick walls.

Deduction 2. Removing the staircases: in order to connect the auxiliary spaces in all four units, I modified it into a corridor and created a new outdoor space at its center. Accordingly, the wooden door and window frames were taken down to create this sense of the outdoors in the space that links the new northern and southern courtyards. After a complete structural reinforcement, only two out of four staircases along the northern corridor were kept—specifically, the staircases on both ends were kept in place, while the two central ones were demolished to form the lofty atrium. Additionally, after the demolition, solid red brick walls were erected on four sides along the original walls to create an echoing space for the water falling from the rooftop canal system.

Deduction 3. Transformation of the garage: several annexes were left in place on the northwest and northeast corners of the main building. One of the largest annexes was a garage, which was 10 meters long and 4 meters wide. The garage was defined as the main space in the northern yard and was used to create a pavilion-like space into which light and water would flow from all directions. With the opening of a skylight on the roof, entering water would be channeled into the central pool, generating a dramatic spatial atmosphere.

Ruin-like courtyard

1 / 2 | 3

1. Water canal
2. Backyard
3. Pavilion

Addition 1. The canal system: after the decision was made to use red bricks as the main construction material, it became important to find an appropriate form to refill and vitalize this ruinous scenery marked by the deduction strategies. After extended brainstorming, an iconic elevated canal system was built on the rooftop. Constructed with small red bricks from the nearby city of Zhuji, this east–west oriented canal functions like a backbone, unifying the entire space. Following the layout of the flue pipes from the four living units, the water from the canal is distributed into four casted concrete diversion channels. From the roof, the water flows down into newly erected beam-like canals, which are one story high. Finally, they lead into a north–south oriented pool of water on the north side of the building. These four new canals, which are about 3.3 meters high, divide the original courtyard into five sections, organizing the space and acting as a metaphor for the local houses known as Taimen, literally translating to "elevated gate."

Addition 2. Log cabin on the rooftop: after the canals on the rooftop had been completed, a log cabin was built under a tree in the roof's eastern corner. It forms a diagonal relationship with the garage gallery on the ground floor. The design of the roof utilizes a system of U-shaped steel plates with 300-millimeter intervals to create cracks of light. To a large extent, this wooden pavilion adds a sense of elegance to the flat roof.

The building's water network is not just a cosmetic addition—it serves as its central system. All of the building's exterior functional spaces and ancillary elements can be understood as plugins to this system. They are integrated according to different needs and can be changed at any time. Ultimately, the selection of features—such as the red brick walls—topographic changes, and the different plants have only one premise, which is to create proper interaction and coordination with the central water system.

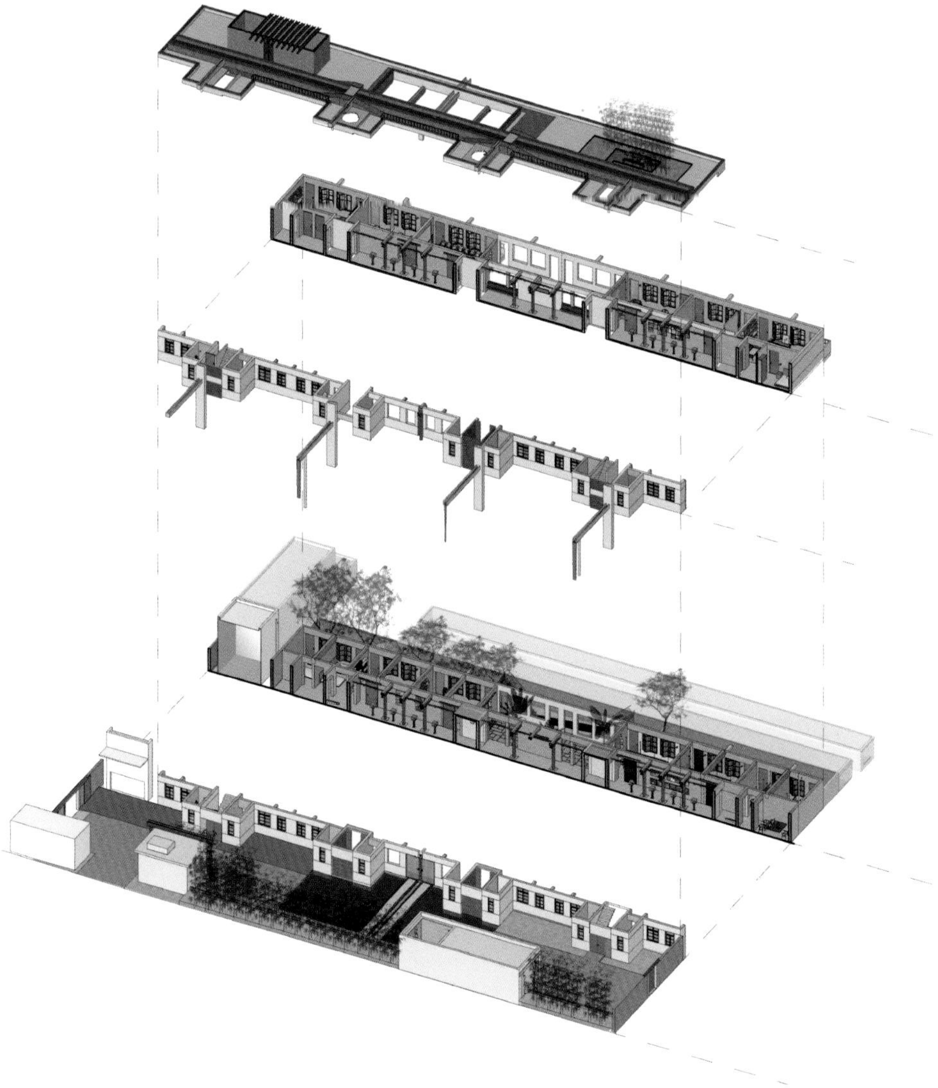

Axonometric diagram

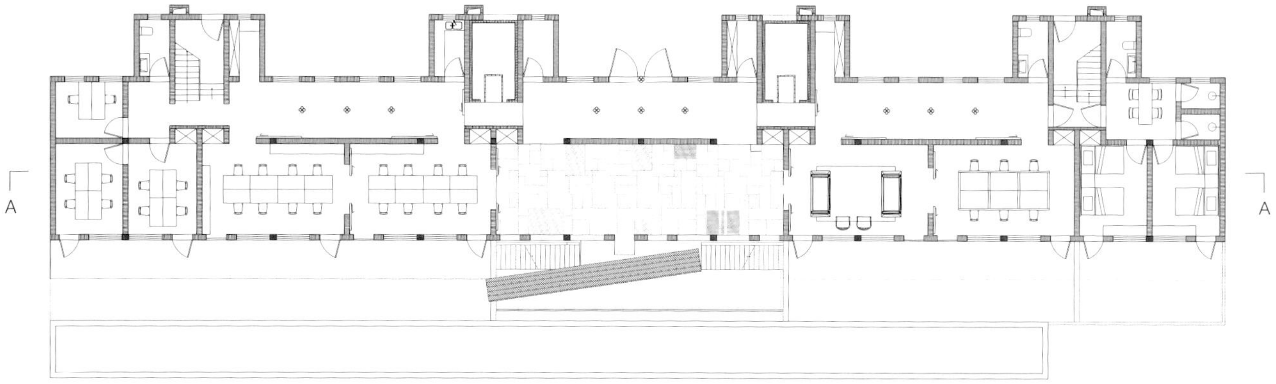

Ground-floor plan

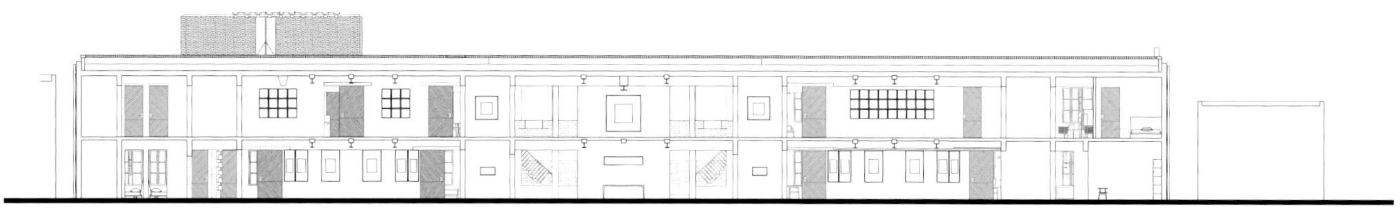

Section A-A

RÙN INN

Location: Qiantong Ancient Town, Ningbo, Zhejiang Province, China
Architect: Untitled Architects
Principal architect: Wang Hao
Design team: Li Wei, Xu Tianxin, Lu Deli, Chen Siyu, Chen Bowen, Han Xinyu
Construction team: Local villagers and craftsmen
Silk scroll maker: Shi Jie
Site area: 150 square meters
Gross floor area: 310 square meters
Design period: April 2015–April 2016
Construction period: April 2016–February 2017
Photography: Chen Hao

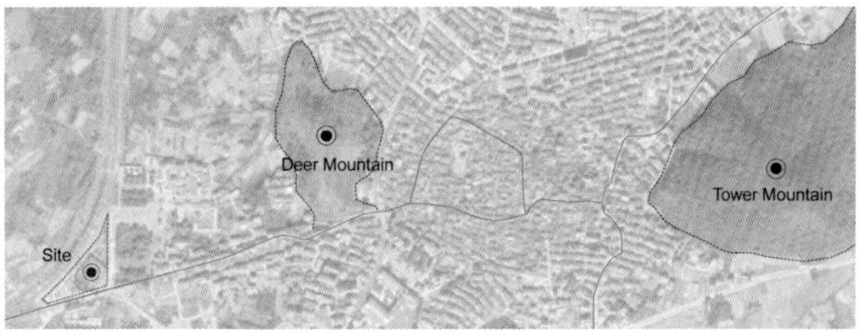

Site plan

Entrance courtyard

Since its founding during the Southern Song Dynasty, the ancient village of Qiantong has been characterized by natural beauty and exceptional inhabitants, both current and former. It has gone unnoticed by the development boom that swept through other ancient villages over the last twenty years, which is, truthfully, a blessing in disguise. After experiencing the destruction brought on by overexploitation and consumerism, the exploration and protection of authentic living has become a new proposition that underlies the development of ancient villages in China, and Qiantong will undoubtedly be a good example to carry out this proposition. For Qiantong, it is important to connect its indispensable local elements in an effort to form a clear and systematic geographical context, and to transcend its own cultural attributes to become a catalyst for a variety of interactions. The "Rùn Inn" project is guided by these concepts.

The many traditional, cultural scenes of Qiantong are synthesized by its buildings. Except for the public ancestral hall, the school, and the house of a former government official, the buildings are houses of common people. Through a logical layout and a sensible drainage system, the houses create an egalitarian and friendly living environment based on common heritage.

Rùn Inn is located in the center of the ancient village. Following the renovation of the courtyard building's brick and timber structure, the inn has been transformed into a culture complex with a clear layout. The redesign and reconstruction of the old building complex extracted the cultural landscape of the surrounding ancient village and reproduced it within. Wood is now the main body to express materiality, while water simultaneously forms the division and connection between spaces.

The design idea began with the beam structure. The studio had in previous projects applied and reinterpreted the typical Qiantong timber structure, so returning to the village, they wanted to put their experiences into practice and looked forward to presenting examples of contemporary residential wood structures that they had come to learn and develop further over the years. While continuing the basic advantages of traditional wood structures, the new Qiantong timber structure subtracts parts of its components. The set-up and deduction of

Entrance courtyard

1. Conceptual drawing of layered beams and columns by silk scroll maker Shi Jie
2. Lounge
3. Guestroom

this structure relies on a deep understanding of traditional architecture, including the integration and combination of new technologies and new materials. Named so by chief architect Wang Hao, the "joist turns pillar" method grafts and replaces the original beams and columns in the way of a "quick pillar," allowing the overall wood structure to comply with a simple and modest contemporary aesthetic.

Rùn Inn also features a *ba-gua* water system that runs from the outside in. At the entrance of the inn, a pond reflects the sky—its reflection naturally changes throughout the day; the pool is not covered, so that rain hitting its surface creates sounds of nature in the inn's artificially created context. An arched stone bridge crosses the pond and reaches the lobby of the inn; at the bridge's end, a waterfall spits out water like a silver gauze, which continues to flow into various areas of the inn's water system. The inn's roof tiles are also replaced by modern glass ones, which enhance the openness of the space with their translucent properties. The water pond and glass tiles echo each other, creating curtains of water and light respectively—one real, one false, one moving, and one still. With their jointed unevenness, materials like wood, marble, brick, and glass create a pulsating visual rhythm between the inside and outside of the space.

In the future, the relationship between Rùn Inn and the outside world will resemble that of a traditional Chinese academy. Apart from the basic function as a homestay, it will serve simultaneously as a diverse three-dimensional living and public space with flexible openness or closeness that can be adjusted according to its actual use. Rùn Inn is determined to gradually become the explorer and accumulator of the ancient town's deep cultural background, leading to the sprout and growth of various creative institutions such as the ancient village's rural library, culture archive, academic seminars, and workshops.

The concept of Rùn Inn reflects the current state of urban economic development, and the actions of people that look back to reflect on their heritage. As technology, the economy, and culture continue to develop, the resources of the big cities and the population from the countryside naturally coalesce to foster rural construction, forming an endless law of reincarnation. Is imagining life in the countryside not one of the most valuable human abilities? Perhaps it is the spiritual homeland that humankind longs for.

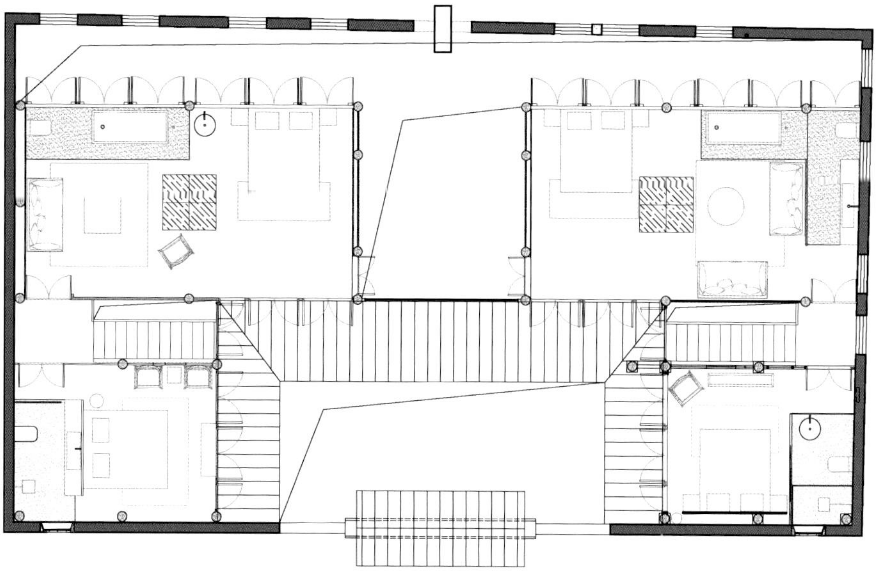

Second-floor plan

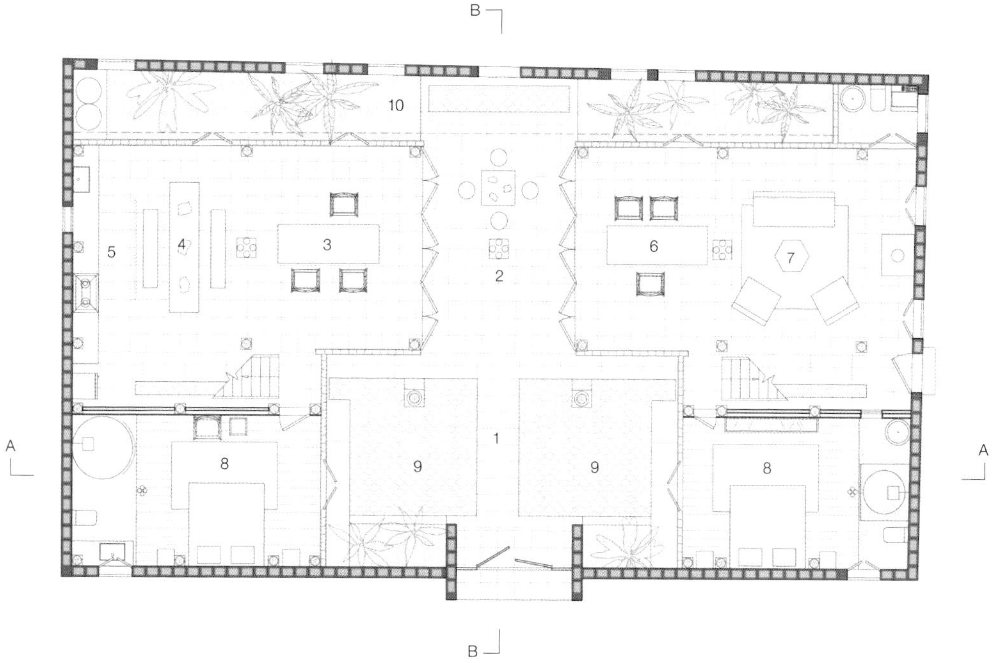

Ground-floor plan

1. Slab bridge
2. Nave
3. Tea booth
4. Dining room
5. Kitchen
6. Study room
7. Living room
8. Bedroom
9. Lotus pond
10. Backyard

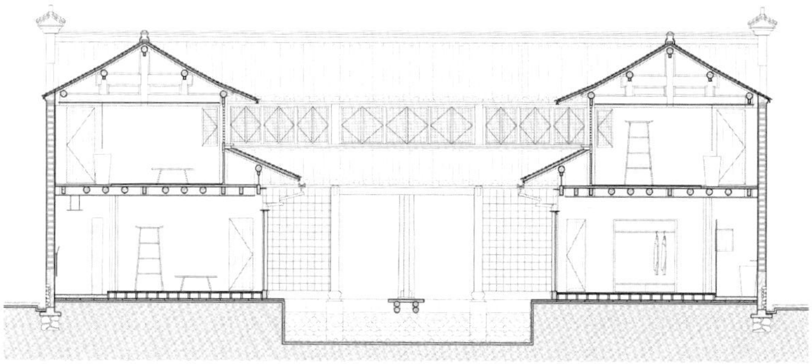

Section A-A

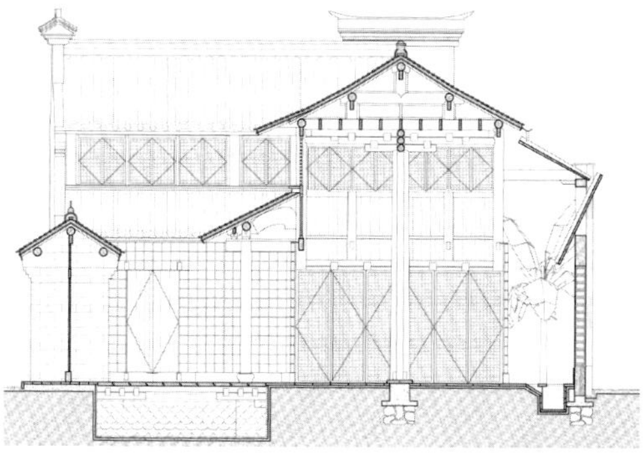

Section B-B

Liu Kenan + Zhang Xu

Atelier XÜK

Atelier XÜK was established in Shanghai in 2010 by Liu Kenan and Zhang Xu who were undergraduate classmates at Tongji University. Liu has a master's degree from Tongji University and previously worked for Herzog & de Meuron in Switzerland, and currently works as a design instructor at Tongji University. Zhang has a master's degree from ETH Zürich and previously, has worked for Buchner Bründler Architects in Switzerland, and currently lectures at Southeast University in Nanjing.

By selecting and combining different types of construction under specific contexts, Atelier XÜK strengthens the characteristics of a specific site and establishes a place.

In the view of Atelier XÜK, "types of construction" is not restricted to the production of spaces and objects, and "characteristics of a site" does not simply mean borrowing or blocking the concurrent views of the here and now. Under specific circumstances, Atelier XÜK discusses and associates these two topics in relation to the transformation of daily lives in regional urbanization processes, as well as the shared memories of people involved in and using the spaces. Atelier XÜK discusses building activities under the context of the process of contemporary urbanization.

Selected Works

2014 Container Showroom, Shanghai, China
2014 Yangzhou Jade Workshop, Yangzhou, China
2017 Renovation of Villa at Columbia Circle on Xinhua Road, Shanghai, China
2017 Sury Hotel No. 3 Moganshan, Huzhou, China
2018 Lostvilla Hotel at Jijiadun, Kunshan, China
2018 Lostvilla Qinyong Primary School Hotel, Ningbo, China
2019 Multifunction Hall and Waterfall Pavilion in Qinglongshan Park, Yixing, China
2019 Waterfall Pavilion, Yixing, China

1/2 1. Sury Hotel No. 3 Moganshan © Chen Hao
2. Swimming pool of hotel © Xu Yifei

Interviewer: Fang Ziyu
Interviewee: Liu Kenan (Liu), Zhang Xu (Zhang)
Editor: Mo Wanli

What is your understanding of "building with nature?"

LIU: I interpret "building with nature" as a fairly broad notion. Everybody understands it differently, so there probably isn't a set conclusion. When you think about "nature" and "building" in conjunction, the first thing that comes to mind is a constructed "natural" setting. Spatial experiences are ubiquitous in nature: the horizon of Lake Taihu, a mountain pass in the Alps, the interior of the karst caves in Wulong—all of these served as models for humankind's earliest construction.

ZHANG: "Building" can be considered a type of separation between humans and nature. All constructions are transformations; they are perpetual. Humans build in order to be liberated from nature, but they also build to return to nature, to a poetic habitat. An example of something close to my understanding of "building with nature" is the Can Lis residence in Mallorca, Spain.

Container Showroom © Su Shengliang

Renovation of Villa at Columbia Circle on Xinhua Road
© Su Shengliang

What are the main directions that your practice is currently exploring?

LIU: Most of my generation was born during the economic reform of the 1980s and grew up during China's economic boom. Our childhood was accompanied by changes like an abundance of material production, the emergence and flourishing of consumerism, redundancy in social productivity, and transformations instigated by the urban setting. These social events and the changes of the times impacted me. I believe that in China today, people's everyday experiences with materials, space, and the city are being covered and iterated at increasing speeds. It's the evanescence of feelings, memories, and emotional experiences. It's the loss of real feelings, of time and memories. I think that's a pity, so we hope to use our own practice to record the current world, or rather, the present that's disappearing as we speak. This is a basic starting point for our work and what we want to achieve. These intentions will be reflected in the many facets of our actual work.

As a tutor, I've introduced the topic of "autobiographical" objects in the course of my teachings at the University of Hong Kong. I wanted students to focus their urban studies on objects in the urban space that have a continuing material lifetime though their usage lifetime has ended. In architectural practice, I have suggested a "recycling strategy." At its core, that strategy is about using basic infrastructures—such as those that are ubiquitous in everyday life but have always existed at the periphery of human consciousness—in juxtaposition with their setting such that their presence is distinctly reinforced; it is also about creating the effect of déjà vu.

ZHANG: Changing project conditions and social settings make it difficult to give meaning to any single work. Unless we can construct a series of perpetual works that changes with time, time will dictate everything. Reflecting on our practices in recent years, it can be seen that our explorations into the definitions of "urbanism" has continued and evolved through the choice of structures, finishing treatment, and construction methods. The multifunction hall at Qinglongshan Park is one example. This structure makes an impact through two types of structural systems: the wide shear wall structure made of fair-faced concrete and the openly installed amenities. This dual structural system allows the multifunction hall to accommodate a variety of activities and encourages people to use the space creatively. In the city, these two structural systems are usually split between large infrastructures and ordinary civic buildings, but not so at Qinglongshan Park. Here, they're merged into a single building because we wanted to create a setting that has a sense of urbanity, density, and tension within the empty mining park. The architecture participates in the urbanized transformation of the space from an empty cavity into a park, and in that, records the present moment.

Lostvilla Qinyong Primary School Hotel © Chen Hao

What are the greatest challenges and opportunities facing young architects today?

LIU: The biggest opportunity is also the biggest challenge, as there is no ready-made path and it takes time to figure it out.

The opportunities arise from the current turning point of China's urbanization: The slowdown in the creation of space and the popularity of the internet have, to a certain extent, influenced the top-down flow of resources in traditional industries. Architects, especially the younger generation, have to face this dilemma in their practice. In a time when monumental structures and showrooms can no longer effectively attract the resources from the top to help realize individual architectural ideals, and when the virtual space proves to be a more efficient means of communicating with the public than the physical space, what is the way forward for architecture studios?

It is clear that our practice does not provide a holistic answer. But we are born into this environment and in order to survive, we have to improve internally and externally. Generally speaking, the external refers to cooperating with space operators and accompanying them to the city or the countryside in order to acquire projects. The internal refers to the design, where we have to aim for a "de-authorized" daily atmosphere and respect the individuality of the users.

Both the internal and external aspects are reflected in the specific projects and require different actions. In retrospect and in conclusion, all of them are closely related to the aforementioned challenges and opportunities.

Guest room in Lostvilla Qinyong Primary School Hotel © Chen Hao

MULTIFUNCTION HALL AND WATERFALL PAVILION IN QINGLONGSHAN PARK

Location: Dingshu, Yixing, Jiangsu Province, China
Architect: Atelier XÜK with Architects & Engineers Co., Ltd. of Southeast University
Principal architect: Zhang Xu, Liu Kenan
Design team: Sun Wenliang, Xi Chao, Zhou Qing, Xu Yifei, Bian Yongwei
Gross floor area: 7,700 square meters (multifunction hall)
Completion: 2019
Photography: Xu Yifei

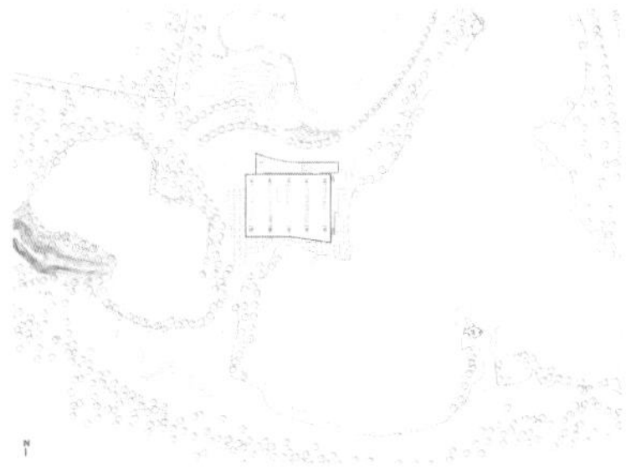
Site plan

Multifunction Hall and Waterfall Pavilion in Qinglongshan Park

Decades ago, Mount Qinglong was the highest mountain in Jiangsu Province's Dingshu area. It was covered in bluestone, which covered a stratum of yellowstone connected to the Huanglong Mountain to the east. It was this yellowstone that contained purple Zisha clay, the raw material for the famous traditional Chinese teapot known as Yixing ware. Even though the earlier inhabitants of the pottery capital, Yixing, had mined clay here for centuries, the mountain retained its ancient features because the impact of that mining was low; though incessant, the mining had a negligible effect on the mountain.

However, things took a ruinous turn in the late 1980s when Mount Qinglong was hit by large-scale mining that went on into two decades after that, up to the turn of the century. This mechanized mining razed the meters-high mountain peaks to the ground and delivered two gaping pits. One quarry was created by a state-owned cement factory in Yixing, which was preceded by a Shanghai garrison-operated quarry, and the second, by the Qinglongshan Cement Factory. Both these pits were subsequently transformed into the deep bodies of water found in Qinglongshan Park today.

According to a local historian, Zong Weifang, the roads around the mining site would be sealed off around 10 am every day and the mining companies in the area would then start setting off explosions. The sounds were deafening and nearby residents could even feel the rocks sundering and cascading down—the sounds of nature's destruction. The quarries were arid at that time, their four walls dagger-sharp and running a bone-chilling height of over 10 meters, from the mountain top to the bottom of the mining pit.

With its rapid development over the last twenty years, Dingshu Town has reached greater heights and seen greater density. The construction of Qinglongshan Park is another notch of achievement in their urban progress. A once old and manual-labor-heavy site, it has been transformed into a Utopian escape for city residents—the early years of large-scale mining has gifted the park with a breathtaking landscape, and accumulated rainfall created the idyllic landscape of the park. Positioned on the former mining site, the architecture not only emphasizes the connection between the city and the landscape, but also between the artificial and the natural.

Entrance to the multifuction hall

The multifunction hall and the waterfall pavilion, together with the towering rocks to the west, help dictate and create the core landscape of the park. The hall is perched atop a massive, exposed megalith. Its west entrance square is adjacent to the rock mass that borders the two mines, and which forms a land bridge; it is the only crossing that connects the southern and northern sections of the park. The main body of the structure comprises shear walls made of fair-faced concrete. The space inside is as wide as four basketball courts. The 38-meter-span of the column-free hall, which was built from prestressed reinforced-concrete can be used for tournaments and exhibitions.

The hall has a clear height of 9 meters, of which 2.7 meters sit below the ground. On the one hand, this design constrains the height and size of the hall to its immediate context. On the other, it frees up the space. The buildings below the megastructure are made of single-layer concrete frame structures enclosed in locally produced terra cotta panels. These building volumes provide spaces for catering, working, meeting, management, and other functions. The fair-faced concrete and terra cotta represent the two local mineral resources that have long supported Dingshu's production and livelihood: limestone and purple clay.

Through the combination of the independent megastructure and an arrangement of single buildings, the building reflects a unique phenomenon in urban space in China's urbanization: the conflict and symbiosis—specifically in terms of materials, structures, composition, and scale—between civilian buildings and large-infrastructure projects that are intended to upgrade a city, such as elevated highways. The building provides the park with a sense of compactness, depth, and urbanity, while the space assumes a dominant role. The low ceiling perfectly complements the distant mountain range and city skyline.

The waterfall pavilion is across from the multifunction hall, set on top of a rock that reaches toward the center of the water. This reinforced-concrete structure takes the shape of a sculpture, one composed of trapezoidal plates, pyramids, and inverted pyramids. Through combination and evolution, the design creates a paradox: simple and elusive, stable and dynamic, artificial and natural. The upper diamond-shaped body opens at both ends of the pavilion, with one end everted, blurring the boundaries and the experiences of the indoors and the outdoors. The transition from vertical to horizontal, and sealed to open, suggests the path of the water.

If the multifunction hall is meant to honor culture, nature, and local history, then the creation of the waterfall pavilion represents a study of artificially made nature.

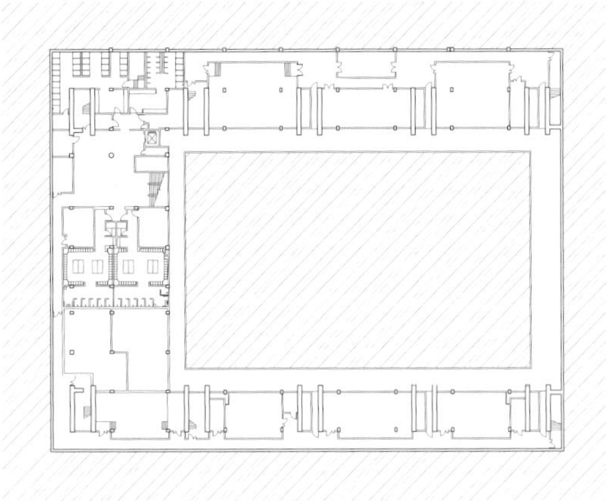

Basement floor plan

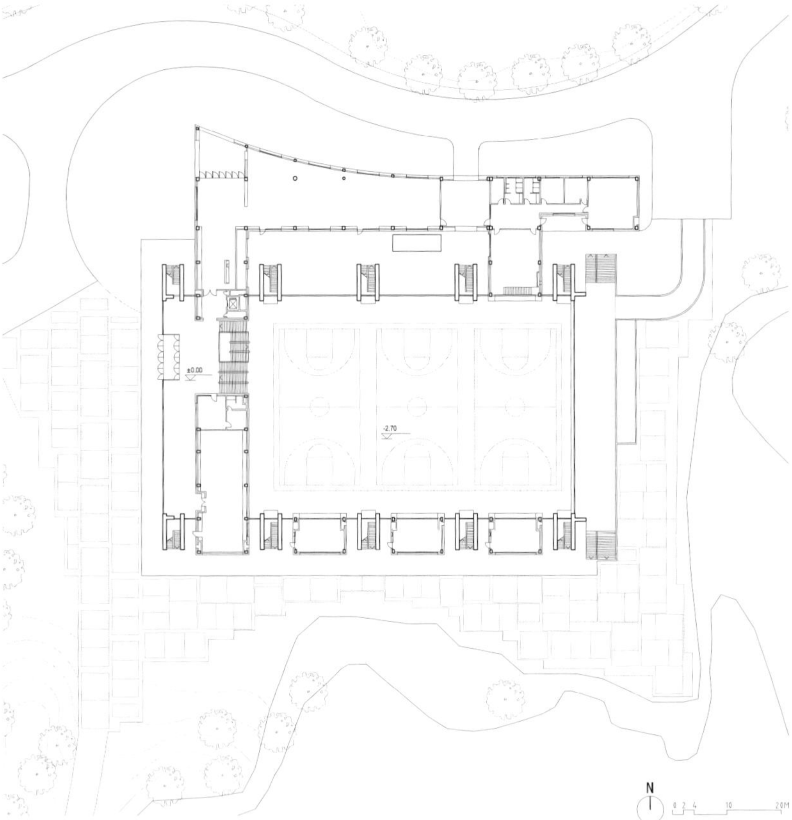

Ground-floor plan

1/2

1. Model of the multifunction hall
2. Interior of the multifunction hall

Waterfall pavilion

Model of waterfall pavilion

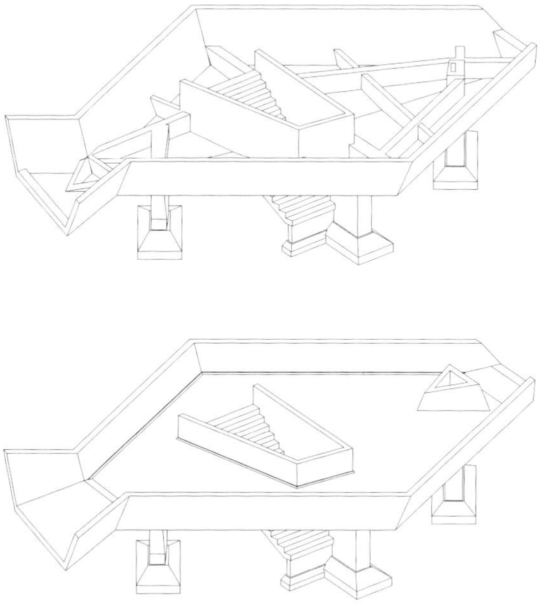

Axonometric drawings of structure

JIJIADUN LOSTVILLA HOTEL

Location: Jijiadun, Jinxi, Suzhou, Jiangsu Province, China
Architect: Atelier XÜK
Principal architect: Liu Kenan, Zhang Xu
Design team: Li Ang, Wang Yekai, Xu Yifei, Shi Xiaoxia, Sha Weiqi
Structure design team: Miao Jianbo, Chen Tong
Mechanical design team: Yu Xiaoming
Gross floor area: 1,300 square meters
Design period: June 2016–November 2018
Completion: November 2018
Photography: Chen Hao

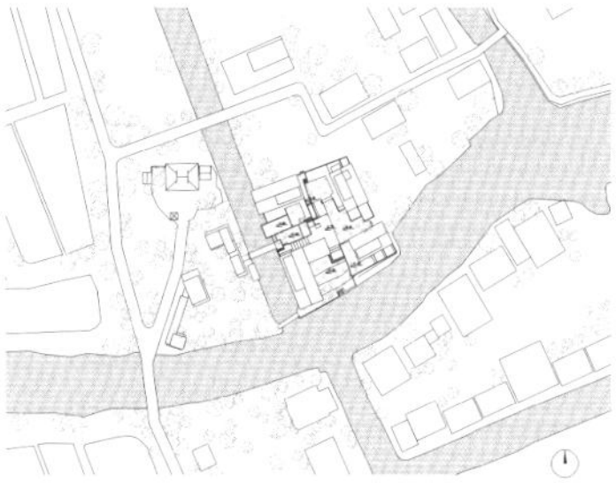

Site plan

Entrance

Jijiadun Lostvilla Hotel is located on the west edge of Jijiadun Village, Kunshan. The village sits on the perimeter of the Dianshan Lake water system; the water network reaches out in all directions throughout the village.

The village doesn't have a long history. Most houses were successively built after the People's Republic of China was established. Under the influence of the rural homestead policy, these houses have turned out uniform in size and appearance. For example, most of them are roughly 150 square meters in projection area, two stories in height, and have stucco walls and double-sloped tile roofs of wood structure. These volumes were considered for the project.

Small rivers flow through the south and west sides of the site. Across the river to the west, is a dense grove of camphor trees, and further away, boundless rice fields. To the north and east of the site, there are other hotels under construction. Given this context, it was essential to block unpleasant and unstable landscape factors when opening up to scenic landscapes, making the overall layout vitally important.

The total area of the project reached 1,300 square meters; it included twenty-four guestrooms and four public lounges and kitchens distributed across four buildings, which fan out in a circular layout.

The density of the guestrooms demanded parallel considerations along three different scales: the scale of the village, the scale of the hotel compound, and the scale of the rooms' interiors. In these three scales, privacy, view, and experience were studied simultaneously during the process of design.

To be specific, at the village scale, it is necessary to take care of the first impressions as visitors enter the site from all directions. At the hotel compound, scale, the visual experience of the outdoor space needs to be coordinated, in terms of what scenery should be captured and what should be blocked. At the rooms' interior scale, a precise balance needs to be reached between interior privacy and landscape. To achieve this, a dynamic relationship between the scenery of the front, middle, and background is established at all the three scales. The layout of the buildings was also developed simultaneously within these three tracks, including massing, interior, and micro topography, which was stabilized gradually during the design process.

In the selection of the construction system, this project does not simply "scan and reproduce" the traditional residences adopted in the region of Yangtze River Delta. Take, for example, the masonry walls of brick and stone and the wooden-structure roofs: the construction adopts the low-cost industrialized building materials commonly used in villages at the

Courtyard

moment, such as concrete beam-column structure and light-gauge steel. The project also takes advantage of the fine local woodworking traditions that still exist: the doors, windows, and interior furniture are made on-site. These choices are intended to echo the current rural landscape, while evoking sentiments that resonate with contemporary urban immigrants who are the potential customers of the hotel.

The adoption of the hybrid construction system is not merely a response to the constraints of a modest budget and the inaccessibility of suppliers in the rural context. For example, the expressive steel-structure balconies are highlighted in the design on purpose to improve the overall experience based on building quality, and to respond to the inaccurate on-site masonry work in rural construction. The application of site-made woodwork to the building envelope, interior partition, and indoor furniture not only fully utilizes the advantages of on-site fabrication in the rural area, it also creates graduations of multiple-layered spatial experiences to expand the cognition of boundaries of both the outdoor and indoor space.

Lounge

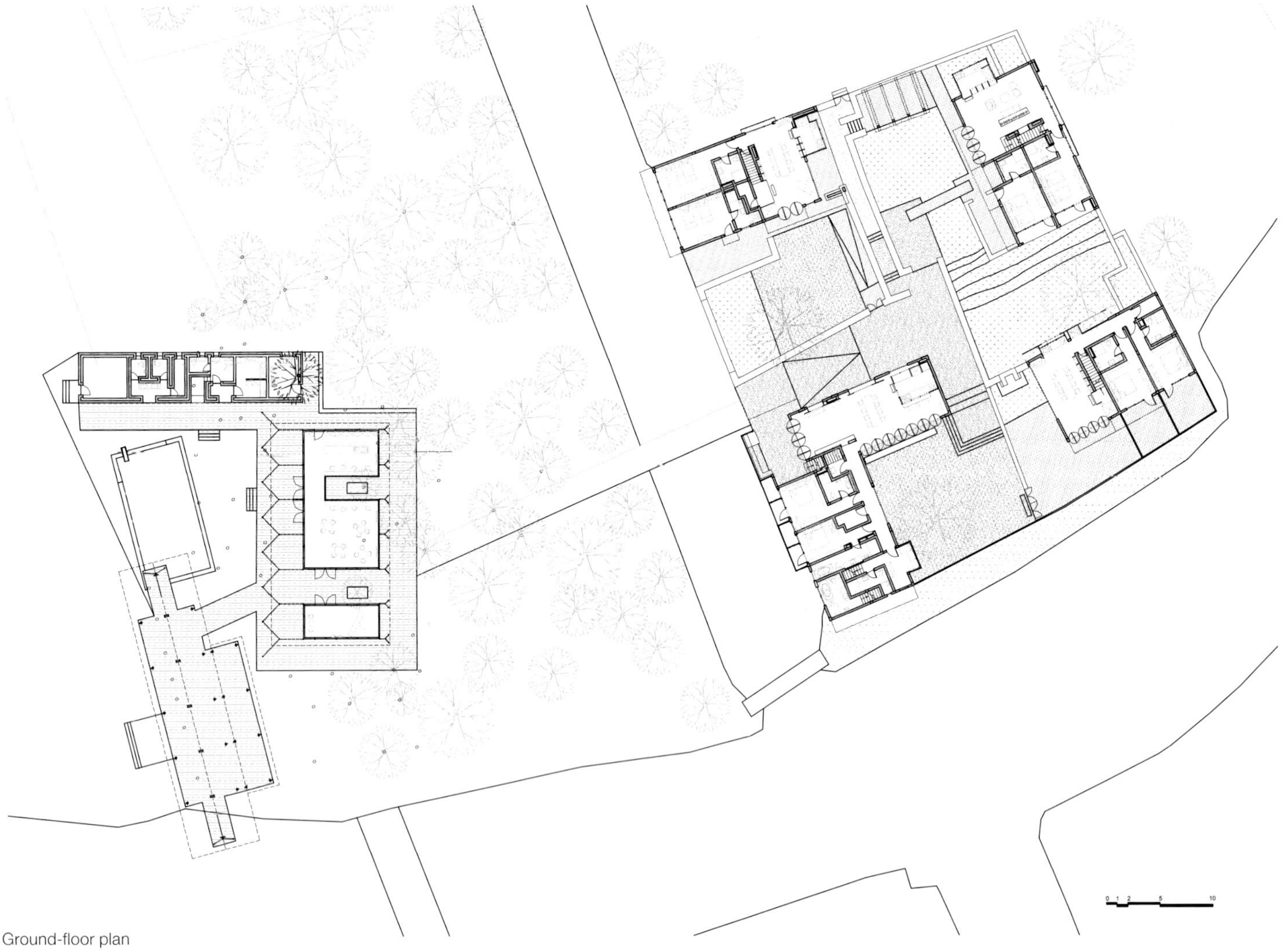

Ground-floor plan

Section

0 1 2 5 10

West elevation

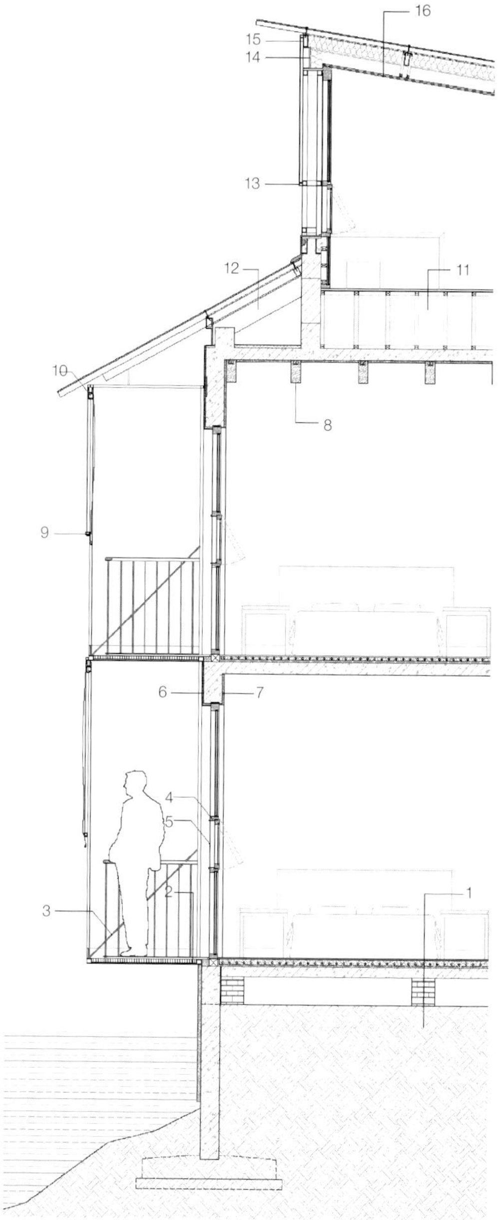

Section detail

1. 12 mm composite wood floor moisture proof pad
   50 mm C15 fine aggregate concrete screed with heating pipe aluminum foil
   50 mm flame-retarded XPS
   1.5 mm polyurethane vapor barrier
   20 mm 1:3 mortar leveling course
   100 mm prefabricated concrete slab
   brick cushion block
   rammed earth
2. Preservative-treated timber floor ends closed by flat stainless steel
   stainless steel grading plate fixed on 50×50×3 mm steel angles
3. Ø16 mm steel hanging rod
4. Pine wood window
5. Fixed wooden frame screen
6. Curing agent
   6 mm 1:2.5 cement mortar, broom finished with horizontal lines
   12 mm 1:3 cement mortar base layer, broom finished polymer cement mortar
7. Latex paint surface
   15 mm 1:2.5 gypsum mortar base layer flatened neat cement, broom finished
8. Decorative timber beam
9. 30×30 mm square steel frame with aluminum paint
10. Bamboo curtain hanged on 30×30 mm steel frame
11. 12 mm composite wood floor
    18 mm blockboard
    elevated wood joist (installed with air conditioner)
12. Corrugated cement fiber roofing panel fixed onto steel purlines with galvanized nails
    vapor barrier
    12 mm OSB board
    T-shaped steel
13. Metallic mesh curtain
14. Steel channel with aluminum paint
15. 130×50 mm square steel beam with aluminum paint
16. Corrugated cement fiber roofing panel fixed onto steel purlines with galvanized nails
    vapor barrier
    12 mm OSB board
    60 mm XPS board
    wood joist
    T-shaped steel
    12 mm blockboard base layer
    12 mm plywood board bottom aligned wirh T-shaped steel

Liu Chang + Gao Qin + Kong Dezhong

Atelier Sounding Architecture

Founded by Liu Chang, Gao Qin, and Kong Dezhong in 2016, Atelier Sounding Architecture aims to combine professional practice and academic research. The three partners share the same academic background: bachelor's and master's degrees obtained from Southeast University in Nanjing, followed by another master's degree from the Accademia di Architettura di Mendrisio (AAM) in Switzerland. Having gathered professional experience through work at Swiss architecture offices like Mario Botta and teaching stints at well-known architectural colleges in China, the atelier began its own explorations into urban planning and building and landscape design. Atelier Sounding Architecture focuses on how buildings, with their physical and material aspects, can fit within the context of a place, stimulate specific behaviors and experiences, and connect with the natural landscape, thus creating a kind of emotional space and initiating a dialogue with the surrounding world.

Selected Works

2015 Vertical Courtyard House, Chuanxing Town, Xichang, China
2017 Visual Art Center of RIA Campus, Rugao, China
2018 Pavilion in Jiangning Sports Park (proposal), Nanjing, China
2019 Qian Fen Xi Rural Center for Social Aesthetics, Pingnan, China
2019 Four Landscape Mediator for a Waterside House, Nanjing, China
2019 Studio Renovation for Atelier Sounding Architecture (built), Hangzhou, China
2019 Kindergarten in Xigang Community (under construction), Nanjing, China
2019 Tianzhongtang Culture Center within Field (under construction), Xianju, China

1
2

1. Exterior view of Tianzhongtang Culture Center in Xianju Town
© Atelier Sounding Architecture
2. Interior view of the Culture Center
© Atelier Sounding Architecture

Interviewer: Fang Ziyu
Interviewee: Liu Chang, Gao Qin, Kong Dezhong (ASA)
Editor: Mo Wanli

What is your understanding of "building with nature?"

ASA: "Building with nature" is to build in response to nature, responding to the laws of nature, the yearning for nature, and the natural humanity. The setting of traditional Chinese residences is a classic example of "building with nature." In our culture, there are also types of nature that are thought of as ideal to stimulate visions of a richer, broader natural world. Today mechanisms of society and our lifestyle have produced drastic changes, as such, architects need to be more proactive in intervening with nature. "Building with nature" means to energetically build a dialogue between people and nature, evoking poeticism in everyday life.

Qian Fen Xi Rural Center for Social Aesthetics © Atelier Sounding Architecture

What are the main directions that your practice is currently exploring?

ASA: Since coming back to practice in China from Switzerland, where we studied and worked, our efforts are directed toward "contemporary localization," which is about preventing the rigid attitude of mechanically borrowing ideas and avoiding nostalgia. We don't have a set answer, methodologically speaking, and every project is different, which really makes it experimental in a way. But the goal we're after is quite clear. Localization shouldn't be a kind of cultural symbol. Rather, it involves the rich, thought-provoking relationship between form, materials, structure, and construction of architecture, as well as factors like site, atmosphere, activities, and perceptions.

Take the art center at Qianfenxi Village in Pingnan: though a renovation project, our consideration went beyond the detailed relationship between old and new on the site, lying in the overall spatial role, on a much larger scale. The project is located at the end of the bridge that enters the old village of Qianfenxi on the other side of the river. We took the project site as a miniature version of an open settlement and reconstructed its spatial order through newly built interventions. This fulfilled the functional uses of the art center to satisfaction and naturally connected the village entrance to the landscape around, demonstrating the characteristics of this place. Every elevation difference hints at the orientation of the spaces, which is also related to the conception of the roof directions, the weight of the materials, and the dimensional rhythm of the buildings. The extensive and very clear transformations of the buildings at the project site also evoke a kind of forked, labyrinthine spatial recollection similar to the old village. As the project neared completion, a number of villagers said that the once crowded site looked more spacious, despite the additions made to the original buildings. Hearing that gave us a great deal of satisfaction.

Through this case, we want to show that a static and unassuming site can exceed our preconceived notions. As we understand it, the various dimensions of the site's clues present themselves as multi-layered: from visible to invisible, from being distant to being close.

Vertical Courtyard House in Chuanxing Town © Atelier Sounding Architecture

What are the greatest challenges and opportunities facing young architects today?

ASA: Globalization and the internet have broadened our horizons, and allowed us to experience good architecture on-site, and given us access to more voices and information. These are the advantages given to us by the era we live in. However, challenges still remain: Amid the numerous, even excessive, information and sounds, can we hold onto our sense of self, avoid falling for superficiality, and slowly form our own way of thinking and values? This calls for us to be keenly aware of the changes in our lives, face the local reality, and continue opening our minds.

QIAN FEN XI RURAL CENTER FOR SOCIAL AESTHETICS

Location: Qianfenxi Village, Pingnan County, Fujian Province, China
Architect: Atelier Sounding Architecture
Principal architect: Liu Chang, Gao Qin, Kong Dezhong
Design team: Liu Chang, Gao Qin, Kong Dezhong
Structure design team: Li Zhiqiang, Tang Jinbing
Gross floor area: 1,450 square meters
Design period: May 2018–November 2018
Completion: August 2019
Photography: Liu Chang, Gao Qin, Kong Dezhong

Site plan

Site aerial view before intervention

Site aerial view after intervention

The site of the art center is located in Qianfenxi Village, Pingnan County, in the southern Chinese province of Fujian. The village sits across the river, along the the bank, and one needs to cross a bridge to access it. The Qian Fen Xi Rural Center for Social Aesthetics is located near the river, just at the end the bridge. The art center thus becomes a part of the village entrance, which requires it to have an open spatial attitude. Houses surround the site along its two street-facing sides; adding to that, the terrain is low, with about 1.8 meters to the street level of the village. Viewed from the roadside, the complex appears quite hidden. The starting point of the design was marked by striking a balance between the autonomy of the site as an art center and its required openness to the village and the surrounding scenery.

The site originally housed a three-story office building, several brickwork granaries, and a warehouse made of rammed-earth walls. Between these buildings was also a jumble of makeshift sheds. Considering the limited construction budget, it was a great challenge for the design to retain as many of the most durable and usable buildings, while also rebuilding a spatial order. Given the local construction conditions, adopting feasible construction methods also posed a difficulty.

Faced with the aforementioned obstacles, the design strategy moved to introduce a new lounge house design. This strategy is based on a type of sheltered bridge common in the area, known as "corridor bridges" in Mandarin. These sheltered bridges not only serve as river and valley crossings, but also as spaces for a range of public activities like daily worship, festival banquets, or even to just enjoy a shady spot during the summer. Similarly, the lounge house concept aims to include the public in this rural art base. It is both open to the villagers and to art education.

View of lounge houses No. 1 and No. 7 from the riverside

We set up seven groups of lounge houses to form a relationship with the existing venues and buildings. For example, the first lounge house is located at the entrance of the site to solve the height difference to the village road, making it not only the entrance of the art base but also a kind of entrance to the village. The lounge house that corresponds to the exhibition hall can become a semi-outdoor gallery or a space for teaching and evaluating art. The lounge house next to the canteen can be turned into an outdoor restaurant, while the one outside the experts' dormitory can serve as a discussion space for teachers or a space for them to interact with students. These lounge houses not only provide a spatial connection protected against the elements, they also serve as an extension of the indoor functions, stimulating flexible and creative ways for their use.

Considering the very limited construction conditions, material selection, timeframe, and other practical factors on-site, the design incorporates a steel structure system and porous brick as the main material, aiming to build a quality space with these simple components. The corrugated metal sheets used on the roof attempt to form a continuation of the tiled roofs of the old buildings, while also creating a contrast between past and present, light and heavy, and top and bottom. In addition to answering to the mechanical requirements of the build, the steel frame echoes the modules of the old house. Under the thin metal roof, a metal frame is used to outline an internal roof reminiscent of traditional Chinese framework.

In the end, the eight groups of lounge houses, each with its own characteristics, interweave and link the old and the new, forming a continuous winding space that calls for creative uses and activities, while ultimately functioning as an open and versatile arts and cultural center.

Night view of the south courtyard

Gathering in the lounge house

Looking back at the entrance

House within the lounge house used as a restaurant

1
2 | 4
3

1. View of lounge house No. 5 from the riverside
2. Balcony
3. The north courtyard
4. Lounge house No. 4

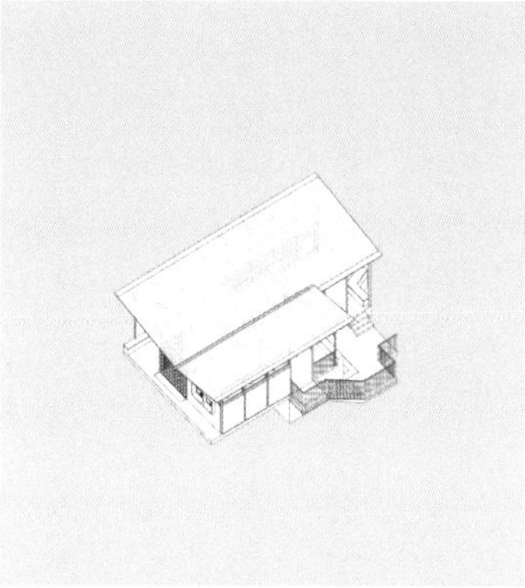

Lounge house No. 1

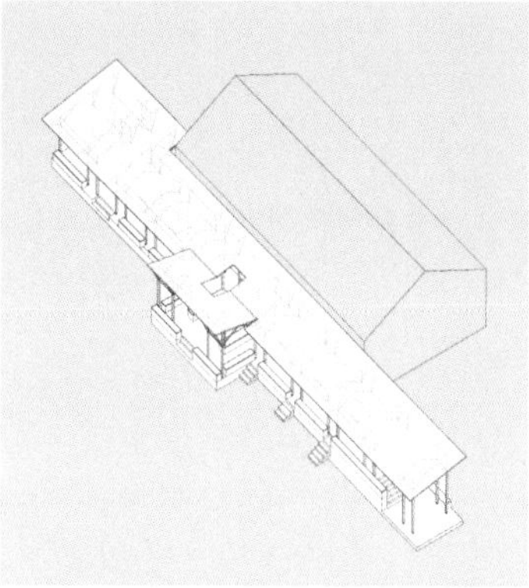

Lounge house No. 2

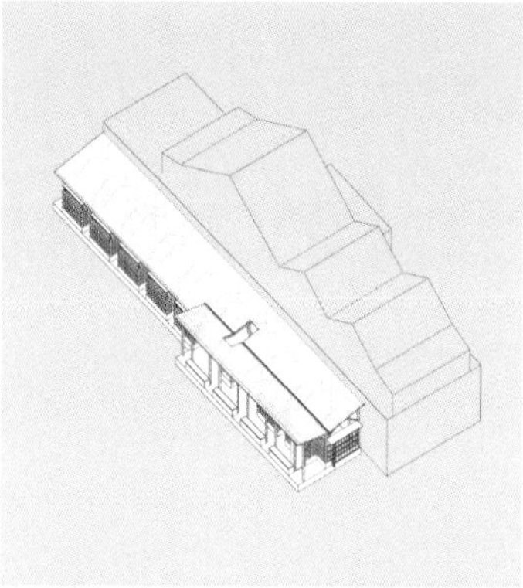

Lounge house No. 3

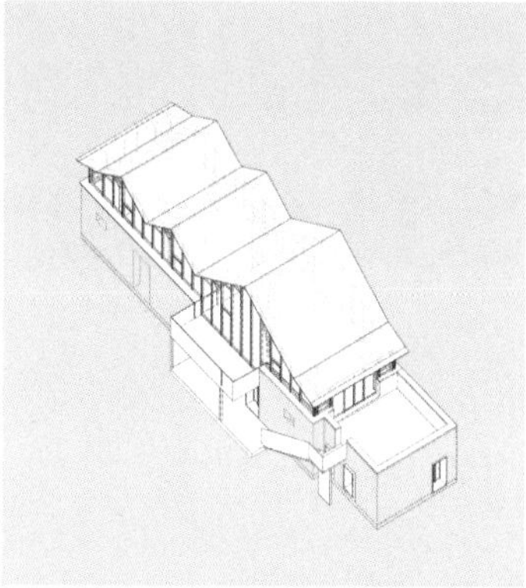

Lounge house room in house

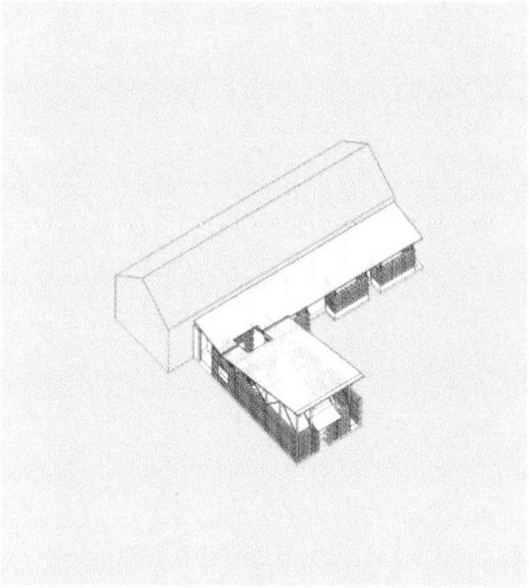

Lounge house No. 4

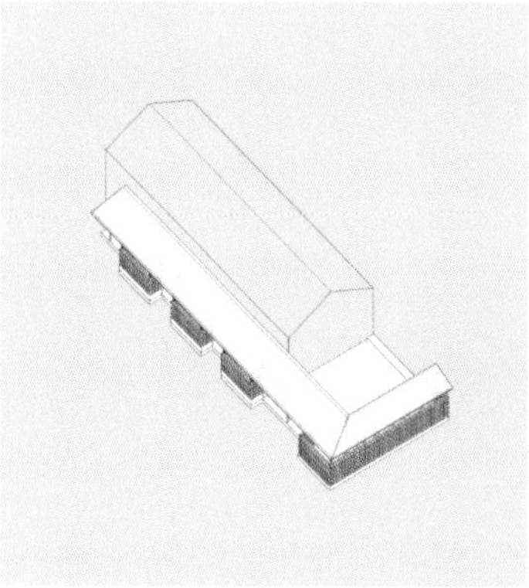

Lounge house No. 5

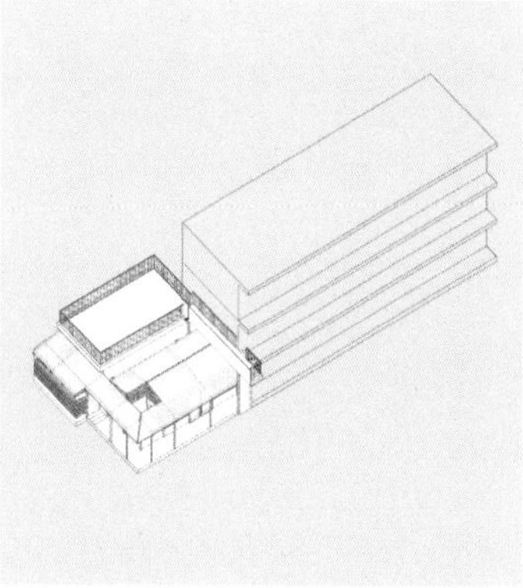

Lounge house No. 6

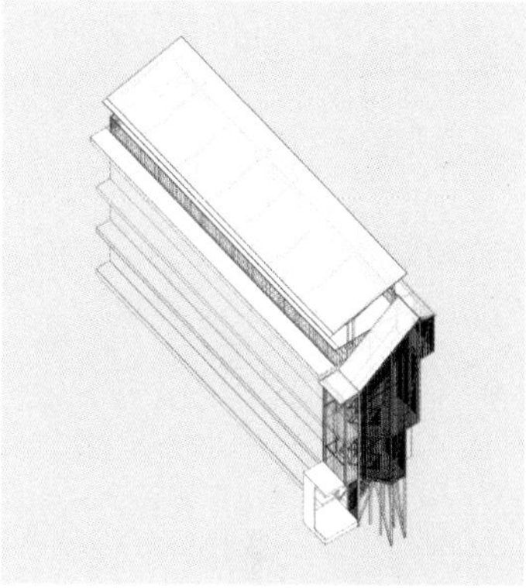

Lounge house No. 7

Axonometric drawings of eight lounge houses

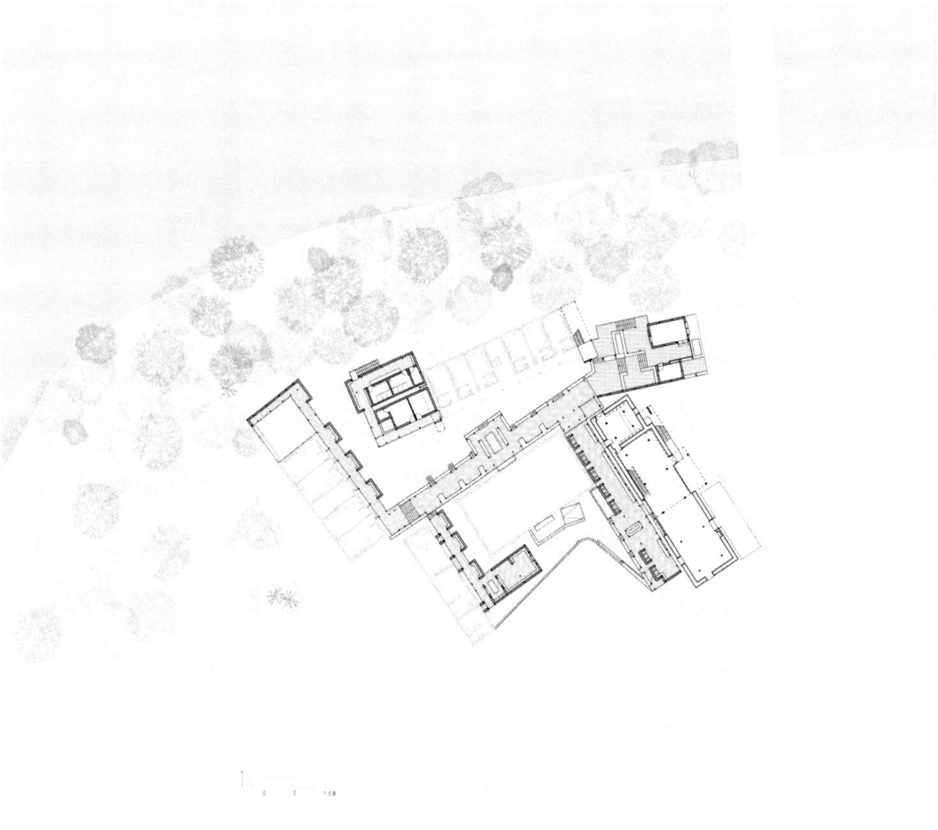

Ground-floor plan

SLIDING SCREEN: STUDIO RENOVATION

Location: Hangzhou, Zhejiang Province, China
Architect: Atelier Sounding Architecture
Principal architect: Kong Dezhong, Liu Chang, Gao Qin
Design team: Kong Dezhong, Liu Chang, Gao Qin
Gross floor area: 77 square meters
Design period: September 2019–October 2019
Completion: December 2019
Photography: Gao Qin

Sliding screen

The original apartment is located at the back of an ordinary multistory commercial and residential compound in Hangzhou. With a floor space of less than 55 square meters, the apartments in this compound are generally quite small, but feature a rather unusual 3.7-meter clear height. For a one story design, this is more than enough, but as a mezzanine-leveled space, it is slightly too small. The lower floor is of standing height, while the mezzanine floor has only enough height to allow sitting or lying down. The two spaces form a complex three-dimensional occlusal relationship reminiscent of Adolf Loos's Raumplan theory; however, they are fragmentary and lack accurate spatial intent. This particular problem of scale became the starting point for the design, which attempts to stimulate an interesting way of using the studio by rearranging the volumes, optimizing the small space, and ultimately creating a diverse and comfortable space for six to eight people.

The core of the transformation strategy is a moving screen, which continues and enhances the apartment's original spatial division. On the west side of the studio, is a large full-height space for communal work with continuous floor-to-ceiling windows in the southwest corner, which let natural light in and add a scenic richness to the space. This aims to create a sense of comfort and freedom different from the typical apartments found here. On the east side, is a series of small auxiliary spaces. The ground floor features a model-making workshop and the bathroom, while the smaller mezzanine space serves as a tearoom and a reading room. All of the rooms and spaces are clearly defined and appropriately scaled through meticulous structuring and grooming.
For example, the reading room on the mezzanine level is created by elevating part of the original floor, creating space below, which becomes a shelf for displaying models. This not only increases the use of space, but also expands the space's boundaries. Additionally, an opening was added to the mezzanine, introducing light from the large space on the west side, allowing for increased interaction between people in the studio.

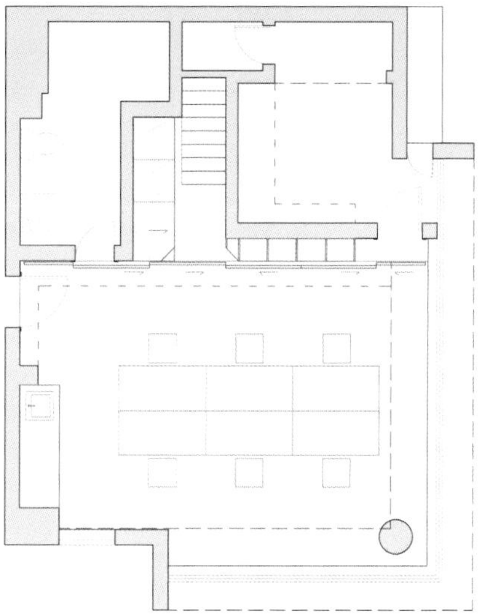

Ground-floor plan

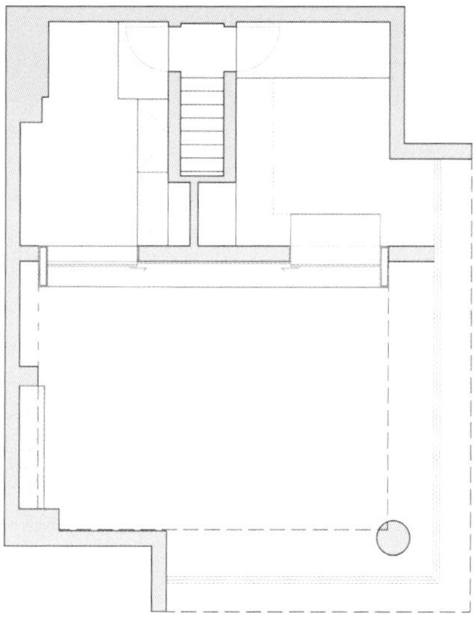

Mezzanine floor plan

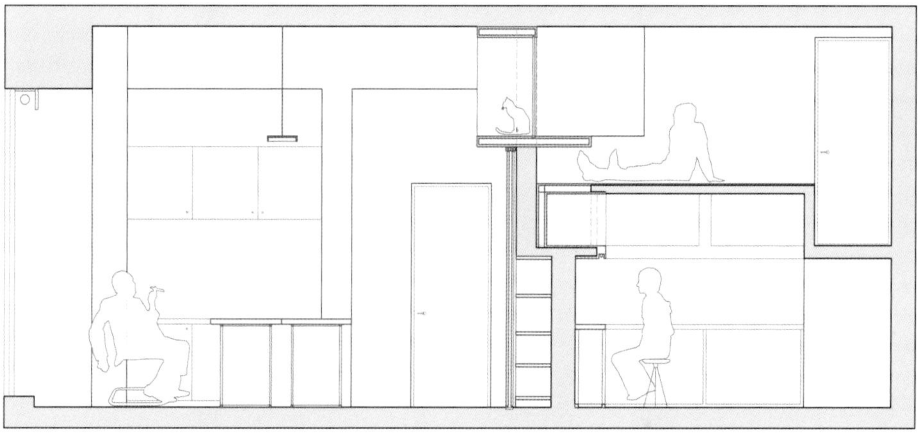

Section

Reading space

The introduction of the sliding screen hides the richness of these smaller spaces akin to a mask. The moving screen is divided into an upper and a lower part. The former hosts a mirror, which visually enhances the large open space. It is also embedded into a thick wooden frame that protrudes from the wall, implying the existence of a room behind the "mask," with its window-like shape. The lower part of the moving screen is composed of a steel plate covered with light-colored linen and can be fully expanded to provide nearly 16 square meters of a magnetic display wall. Both screens are placed on double tracks so that they can be moved and adjusted according to daily requirements. Therefore, different spaces are sometimes open and sometimes closed, sometimes hidden and sometimes revealed. It seems that the spatial organization of the studio can't be easily grasped at first sight, but the sliding screens leave a series of spatial clues and enrich the experience and depth of the space.

Shui Yanfei + Su Yichi

NATURALBUILD

NATURALBUILD was founded in 2012 by Shui Yanfei and Su Yichi. Amid the complex and contradictory reality of contemporary China, NATURALBUILD embraces the Eastern philosophical view of Advaita Vedanta, which believes in the "absence of duality between subject and matter," and that "everything is part of a whole;" an extension of *one* reality. Opposed to functionalism, they reject the dichotomy of binary opposition and aim to transcend the pure concept, where the "focus on the familiarities of everyday life" has become the starting point of the studio's design thinking.

On the one hand, they thoroughly investigate different regions, invoke the ancient heritage and wisdom of local construction, and aim to establish a relatively economic spatial mechanism to gain the freedom of use in response to the increasingly severe challenges of ecology and energy. On the other hand, however, NATURALBUILD also attempts to excavate the possibilities hidden within prevalent industrial technologies and materials, and explore the new potential between body, perception, and environment, which would expand the meaning of naturality in contemporary living.

Selected Works

2011 Tongling Copper Mine Site Museum (under construction), Ruichang, China
2014 1178 Waima Road Warehouse Renovation, Huangpu District, Shanghai, China
2017 Lostvilla Boutique Hotel in Yucun, Huzhou, China
2018 J House, Shanghai, China
2018 RV Campground Club, Shanghai, China
2018 Yushan Summer House I, Suzhou, China
2017 Yushan Summer House II (under construction), Suzhou, China
2017 Soft Matter, Shanghai Urban Space Art Season, Shanghai, China
2019 Shibantai Hotel, Beijing, China

Lostvilla Boutique Hotel in Yucun © Chen Hao

J House © Chen Hao

Interviewer: Fang Ziyu
Interviewee: Shui Yanfei, Su Yichi (NATURALBUILD)
Editor: Mo Wanli

What is your understanding of "building with nature?"

NATURALBUILD: The topic of "building with nature" might hint at a reflection on China's rapid urbanization or point toward a kind of instinctive resistance. Against this backdrop, it only makes sense that the countryside would be at the forefront of "building with nature" and occasionally, even offer us an idyllic vision of the past. In reality, our practice in the countryside in recent years has allowed us to deeply experience the "slowness" that characterized traditional vernacular architecture—a kind of wisdom that grows and adjusts over time. What really surprised us is the horrific juxtaposition of different ideological elements in the countryside today. While we're contending with the spontaneous growth of pragmatic spaces, we're also ushering in a new round of infrastructure construction like power generation, data centers, and logistic hubs. The dichotomy between city and non-city becomes meaningless. The modern lifestyle spurred by China's unprecedented urbanization freely tore through the countryside and all the remaining spaces.

Therefore, our primary work lies in describing the tension arising from this drastic transformation. We delve into different areas, harness the ancient genes and wisdom of local architecture, and seek to establish a relatively economic spatial mechanism that grants us the freedom to respond to the growing ecological and energy challenges of our time. At the same time, we have also tried to tap into the hidden possibilities of popularized industrial technologies and materials, as well as explore the new potential between bodily perception and the environment, and generally expand nature in our modern life.

What are the main directions that your practice is currently exploring?

NATURALBUILD: You might say that our initial attempts developed along two directions: ground nature and plastic nature. People are more interested in the experimental aspect of materials, so our projects like Soft Matter tend to be more prominent. In comparison, the exploration of mechanisms produced by space tend to be less visible. Geography still plays a pivotal role in these projects and we need to adapt to different landscape needs and the relatively fixed boundary of residential sites. In terms of construction logic, such projects operate somewhere between renovation and new construction. Ultimately, we are focused on devising a rational mechanism so as to enable many possible future uses. And these uses are only enabled through providing the fundamental qualities of modern architecture.

For example, with the homestay project in Yu Village at Moganshan, we considered connecting the existing residential sites as much as possible with its surroundings to recreate the experience of wandering and provide more common space for the town. The available space for the summer houses on Yushan Island were more scattered. With the limited funds we had, we had to first establish the extent of the village's public infrastructure (docks, roads, and water supply). We also developed a simple, effective construction system to meet the needs of different people, and the different levels of renovation, which led to subsequent imitations by the nearby residents. In contrast, is the Shibantai Hotel project. The original structure remained relatively intact, enabling us to organize a family-oriented model with multiple clusters and to transform the open-air courtyards into indoor, shared living rooms.

SHIBANTAI HOTEL

Location: Shibantai Village, Xiayunling Town, Fangshan District, Beijing, China
Architect: NATURALBUILD
Principal architect: Shui Yanfei, Su Yichi
Design team: Liu Wenhao, Zou Yongjun, Shi Mingyu, Ye Ying, Deng Weiyan, Yang Yuwei, Zheng Min, Wang Haocheng, Zhang Shuai, Wang Lili, Lou Yin, Chen Tianjian, Zhang Yangfan
Structure design team: Zhang Zhun
Gross floor area: 3,160 square meters
Completion: 2019
Photography: Chen Hao

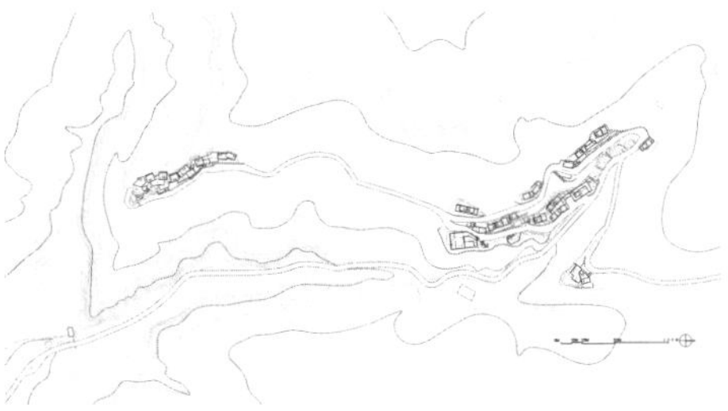

Site plan

Distant view of the hotel

Exterior view with landscape

The project site is located in Shibantai Village in Taihang Mountains, along the western outskirts of Beijing. Although it is only 100 kilometers from the capital, the village's level of development is very different from that of the urban area. A former revolutionary base during the Chinese Civil War, it is known for dangerous mountain roads and extreme poverty. Over the past ten years, China's rural tourism has witnessed an explosive growth throughout the country. Underdeveloped areas with outstanding topography and favorable environments have become hot spots for rural tourism and Shibantai Village is no exception.

This phenomenon reflects a deeper level of societal needs and originates from China's unique land system. Compared to the state-owned land in the cities, rural collectives and homesteads provide the public with private homes or summer houses similar to those which are provided in Western land systems. They allow independent construction or the alteration of the spaces, thus providing an opportunity to the public—notably the generation born in the 1980s and 1990s— to create a lifestyle of their own which differs from the increasingly homogeneous urban living model provided by real estate developers. At the same time, the rapid development of China's internet economy and the formation of online communities over the past decade have spurred the public's recognition of the sharing economy. But contrary to the international crowdfunding platform Kickstarter, the fundraising model in China's rural economy emphasizes co-contribution. This allowed for more people to participate in the construction of this holiday resort at different levels of investment, construction, consumption, and operation. Through crowdfunding, the virtual community realized the idea of this space.

The first challenge in this resort project, therefore, was turning the demand for communal vacations into a physical space. This meant coming up with a unique design different from traditional hotel rooms or private villas that also meets the needs of a diverse range of social and family lifestyles. The Xiayunling area where Shibantai Village is located features a unique geological schist structure. Many local villages use the small and large stone slabs as building materials for house roofs and as retaining walls for terraced fields. The local stonemasonry tradition is thus very well developed and intact.

Unfortunately, when we took over the design, the original Shibantai Village had already been demolished after being abandoned for a long time. So while thinking about new types of structures, we also had to consider the specific characteristics of the site. We did not want to restore

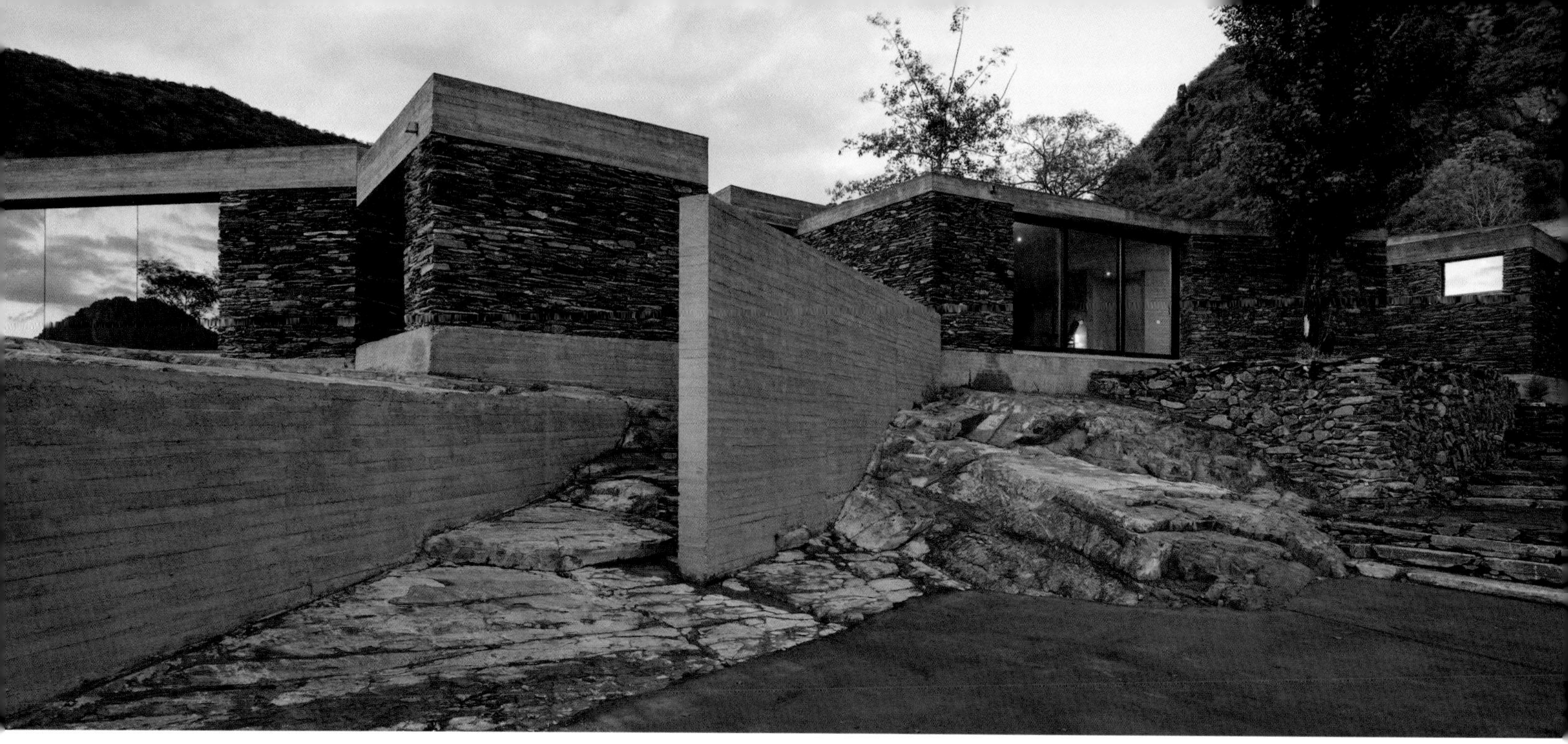

1 — 1. Entrance to the hotel

2 — 2. Wall and rocks

the village's original appearance—objectifying it in a sense—but, instead, wanted to be guided by the local conditions and potential constraints.

We cleared the existing layer of muck from the site to re-establish its relationship with the mountain, obtain a more accurate terrain profile, and make the connection between different elevations and the landscape visible. Adapting to the local terraced farming fields built with stone, we applied a flat roof with a rooftop garden to the design to create a terrace-like spatial quality. Thanks to the abundance of schist as raw material and the local stonemasonry tradition, we also used concrete and schist slates for insulation. They not only provide good physical properties, but also respond to the locality in a range of ways. A width of 400 millimeters is reserved on the outside of the concrete structure wall, with insulation boards fixed to it with expansion bolts. When the layered stone slabs reach the position of these bolts, a steel wire mesh and cement mortar are used to fix the schist in place; the entire façade uses alternating large and small shales. Their rough surface is faced outward to visually echo the overall sense of the mountain shale, while also facilitating the construction of the walls. Considering the relationship with the mountain, we transformed the outdoor courtyards between the original independent guestrooms into internal communal living rooms and reduced their interior floor height. On the outside, they still retain their visual intention as a yard, however, the space gains a multidirectional horizontal extension on the line of sight on the inside. Rooms at different elevations and with different ceiling heights also mimic the experience of the changing mountain profile. We aimed to incorporate the spatial variation of the terrain into the original living rooms, thus diversifying them while also creating a certain pattern throughout the units. This also reflects the exceptional construction and operation of the entire project.

In the end, the topography of the site was extended on the inside and outside of the design through subtle differences in elevation and a precise framing of the scenery. Subdued sunlight reflecting from the yellow concrete carries warmth into the northern Chinese wintery interior. Without the necessity of an outstanding event, experiencing something new in our everyday life becomes common and very "everyday." The design uses the most ordinary things in life and adjusts our relationship with them. By letting our intuition lead, it provides us with surprises.

Ground-floor plan

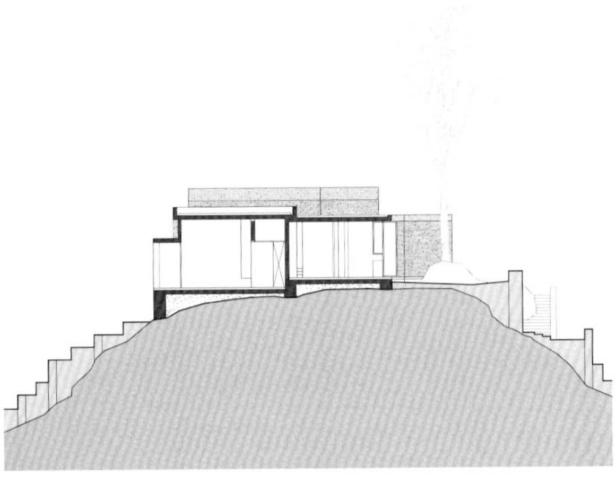

Section A-A

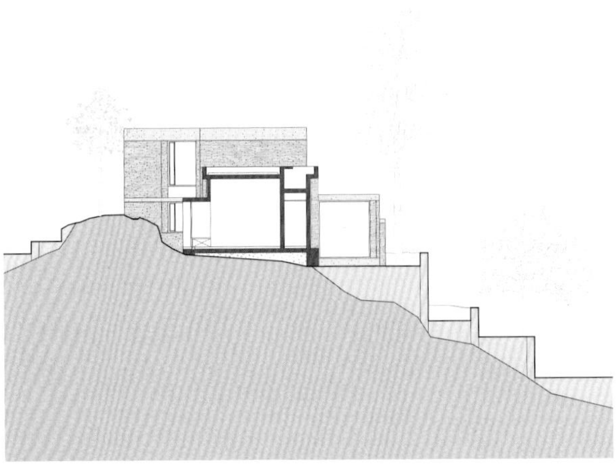

Section B-B

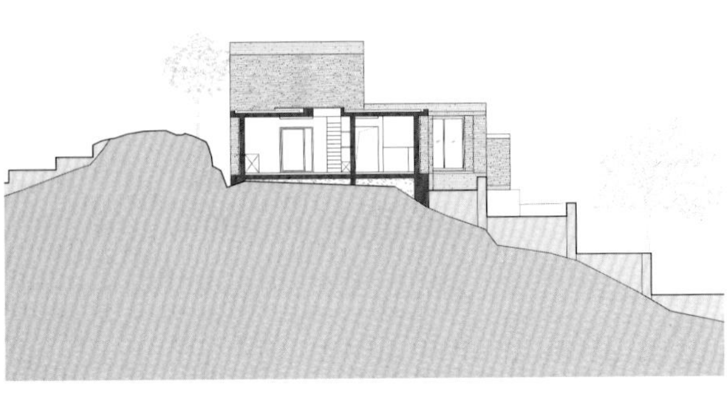

Section C-C

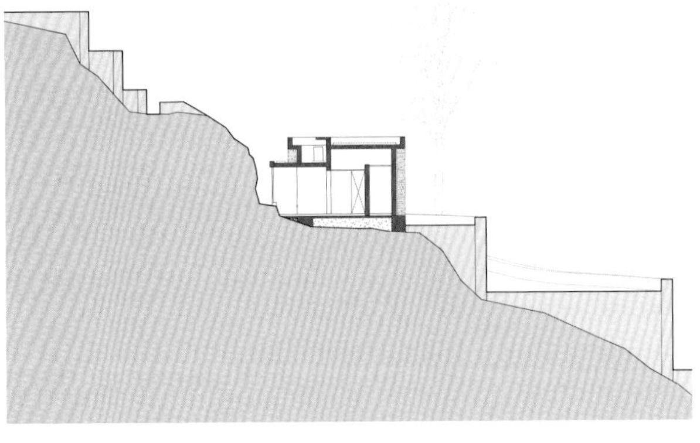

Section D-D

Model

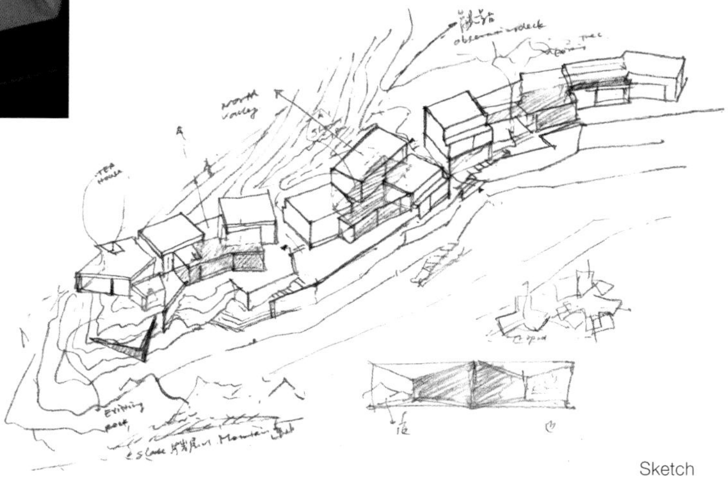

Sketch

Detail

1. Guestroom shower
2. Guestroom vestibule
3. Living room hallway
4. Wood-grained red cast-in-place concrete exterior wall
5. Cyan shale masonry wall
6. 50-mm-thick polystyrene board insulation
7. Cast-in-place (red) reinforced-concrete wall
8. Insulated green roof
9. Drainage gutter
10. Exterior air-conditioner unit platform
11. Fluorocarbon aluminum window
12. Thermal insulation roof
13. Cyan pebble pavement
14. Mountain rock
15. Terrazzo

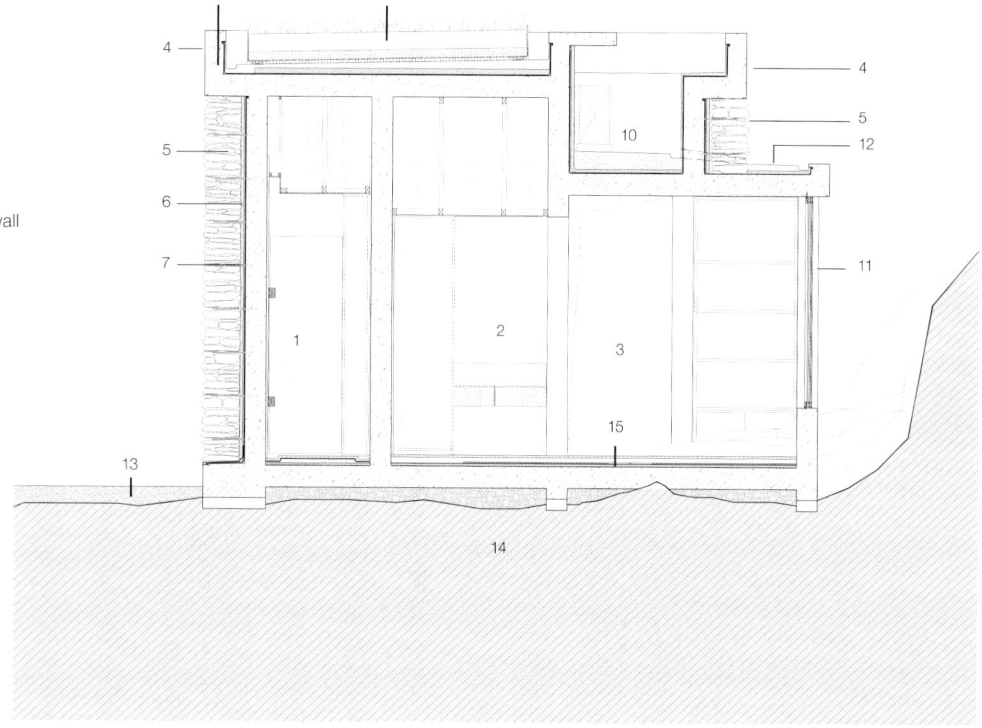

Wang Baozhen

Yinyuan Studio

Founded by Wang Baozhen, Yinyuan Studio focuses the foundation of its architectural designs on tectonics, using the tradition of Chinese gardening, the idea of "places for roaming," and poetic imagination as the means of attuning these designs. In order to fuse Chinese tectonic tradition and contemporary techniques, Yinyuan Studio aims to experiment with a series of correlative factors: materialization, detailing, structural considerations, and atmospheric and bodily experiences.
By seeking a balance among these factors, the studio hopes to create a place with an inspiring atmosphere. The second motivation for their practice lies in reviving the tradition of the Chinese garden. As a kind of an all-encompassing art, the classic Chinese garden should be considered a counterpart to Western architectural tradition, rather than merely a characteristic timber structure system. This great gardening tradition has had—and will continue to have—a positive impact on the Chinese way of life. According to the work of the famous eleventh-century painter and gardener Guo Xi, an ideal garden should be designed as a place "where one can walk, where one can view, where one can live, and where one can roam." While these principles are oftentimes overlooked by Western architecture, they form a guideline for the designs of the studio. The architects also propose a novel form of elementary composition, which is not just based on its visual quality, but also on poetic imagination.

Selected Works

2010 Ellipse Garden, Guangxi, China
2014 Bamboo Pavilion / Tiger Chamber, Guangxi, China
2016 Quzhe Xiao Yuan, Henan, China
2017 Rong Garden, Guangxi, China
2019 Ru Yuan (under construction), Henan, China

Interviewer: Fang Ziyu
Interviewee: Wang Baozhen (Wang)
Editor: Mo Wanli

Ellipse Garden © Wang Baozhen and Weng Zitian

What is your understanding of "building with nature?"

WANG: My understanding of the term involves two main aspects. One is creating a poetic union between man and nature; the second lies in excellent propriety. The principles of traditional Chinese garden design state: their ingenuity lies in borrowing from nature, and their refinement in finding the right balance between objects. Of the two main aspects of "building with nature" mentioned above, the former relates to the goal, while the latter to the means. One example that exemplifies "building with nature" is Feng Jizhong's Helou Pavilion.

What is your current direction for exploration?

WANG: My explorations mainly cover four areas. The first, and the most fundamental aspect, is building. Considering the intersection of traditional Chinese culture and modern civilization, what do we make of the ingenuous interaction between all the factors, and from there, how do we create a touching, thoughtful place to live in? The second aspect is the discourse of the garden: How do we organize and manage the complex, the diverse lives, and the functional requirements of today with the thinking and wisdom of Chinese building—how can the natural and the artificial complement each other? The third, is the idea of an explorable place. In his work *Linquan Gaozhi*, the Chinese painter Guoxi of the Northern Song dynasty proposed four hierarchal criteria for landscapes: it should invite one to roam, gaze, reside, and explore. I see those as the standards of the ideal living environment in China. Against the backdrop of globalization, most designs—Western or Japanese—see "poetic dwellings" as the highest ideal, so they go no further than "roaming, gazing, and residing." Le Corbusier and Frank Lloyd Wright once seemingly had an interest in peering into the "exploring" aspect, though it didn't work. What constitutes as "explorable?" How do we make something "explorable?" The last thing is written culture and gardening. Literature was highly important and fundamental to the traditional literati, so focusing on literature will shed more light on some of the ideas and issues of gardening.

How have traditional Chinese gardens influenced your exploration?

WANG: The Chinese word for a traditional garden contains the two different concepts of "courtyard" and "garden." I'll briefly share what I've learned.

How do you create a real courtyard? Chinese architecture and courtyards emphasize the relationship between yin and yang, between the female and male principles. The key to the problem is finding the right balance. There are a number of traditional techniques to achieve this: connecting, teasing, playing cat and mouse, saying "no" and meaning "yes," and more. The most incredible thing about gardens in China is that they create an explorable space. Our highly mechanical, rapid, and hectic work and living circumstances created a series of physical and mental illnesses, despite our residences being more stable than those of agrarian civilizations. The thinking and methods contained within Chinese gardens remedy these diseases. Therefore, I use the discourse of the garden as the main part of my exploration; an explorable place as the ideal pursuit of my layered narrative; and written culture and gardening as nourishment for my thoughts and methods.

What are the greatest challenges and opportunities facing young architects today?

WANG: Challenges are opportunities. In a society that revolves around technology, while development progresses at a rapid pace, the relationship between humanity and nature becomes increasingly distant. Most designs, even if they are conceptually natural, are just like film sets, stickers, or screensavers. These images are just symbolic notions, flat and transient—they have little connection to the body, except an occasional one with the retina. But how can humankind, as a creature and not a machine, maintain a healthy mind and body apart from nature? This is a question we must consider thoroughly. Otherwise, the act of thinking—constantly driven or shaped by technology—will become what Bertrand Russell called the "refinement of folly." Perhaps there is another kind of architecture, such as garden architecture, that can provide life and vitality to our cities, to our countryside, and to our bodies and minds. Moving toward garden architecture would be another opportunity for us.

BAMBOO PAVILION / TIGER CHAMBER

Location: Guangxi Province, China
Architect: Yinyuan Studio
Principal architect: Wang Baozhen
Collaborator: Chen Haiyi
Gross floor area: Bamboo Pavilion – 160 square meters; Tiger Chamber – 290 square meters
Design period: May 2013–August 2018
Construction period: February 2014–August 2014
Photography: Weng Zitian, Wang Baozhen

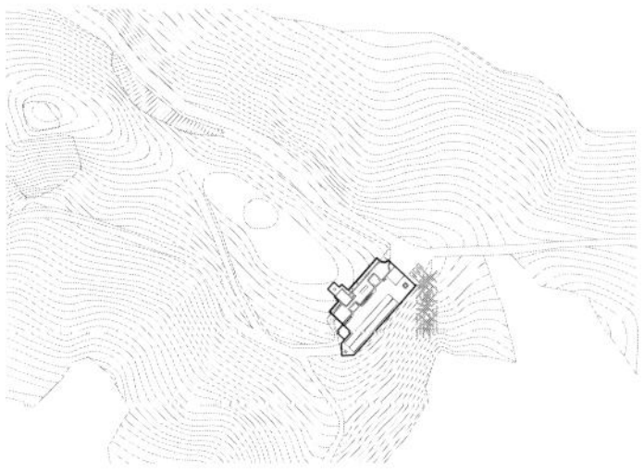

Site plan

Bamboo Pavilion at night

Bamboo Pavilion during the day

Bamboo Pavilion

The magnificent mountain views of southern China inspired the light and open design of the pavilion, which is a favored spot among farm workers to have lunch. In Chinese tradition regarding gardens, borrowing views from the infinite creativity of nature and weaving it into the final construction of a garden surpasses artificially created structures. In a similar vein, Edward E. Casey describes in his book, *Representing Places,* that nature itself is thought of as something that is "within" rather than "without." The famous Tang Dynasty poet, Du Fu, too, makes reference to nature's beauty in a poem describing his home: "My window frames the snow-crowned western mountain scene; my door oft says to eastward-going ships, 'goodbye!'" The light bamboo structure of the pavilion not only frames the view, but also provides a permeable system that introduces the cool breeze and the subtle hues of the mountains into the building.

For the pavilion, we imagined a dense composition of very light, thin, and tall bamboo poles, which resembles a growing grove, while simultaneously bearing the impact of the elements and adapting to them. Resting on top of a small hill looking far into the distance, the pavilion seemingly floats above the forests when viewed from afar. And like a similar pavilion in the *Xiashantu* landscape scroll by Tang Dynasty painter Dong Yuan, the shape of the Bamboo Pavilion is defined through an adaptation of the traditional Chinese column and bracket system.

The pavilion is built with inexpensive local materials: common bricks as foundation, treated moso bamboo for the structure, stainless-steel pipes and screws as joints, and bark from Chinese cedar trees for the roof. Despite not being made to last for eternity, the structure has so far managed to survive two fierce typhoons, emerging without a scratch, bringing to mind one of the messages in the ancient *Book of Changes* that one has to be flexible to confront the unpredictable environment in a constantly changing world.

View of the Bamboo Pavilion through the Moon Gate

Tiger Chamber

Contrary to the lightweight appearance of the pavilion, its counterpart, the Tiger Chamber, is solid and heavy and serves as a storage space and canteen. The walls use the traditional building technique known as "tiger fur wall," which is built from natural rough stones. As part of an enclosed courtyard building, it represents a strong background for the pavilion on the sloped hillside. Like a Chinese poem, the two structures reveal themselves in a contrasting fashion of open and closed, light and heavy, up and down, and shallow and deep. A continuous dialogue takes place between them—one moment you are taking in the view, the next, you've become the view itself.

Rooftop of the Tiger Chamber

Tiger Chamber

Vertical window of the Tiger Chamber

Corner of the Bamboo Pavilion

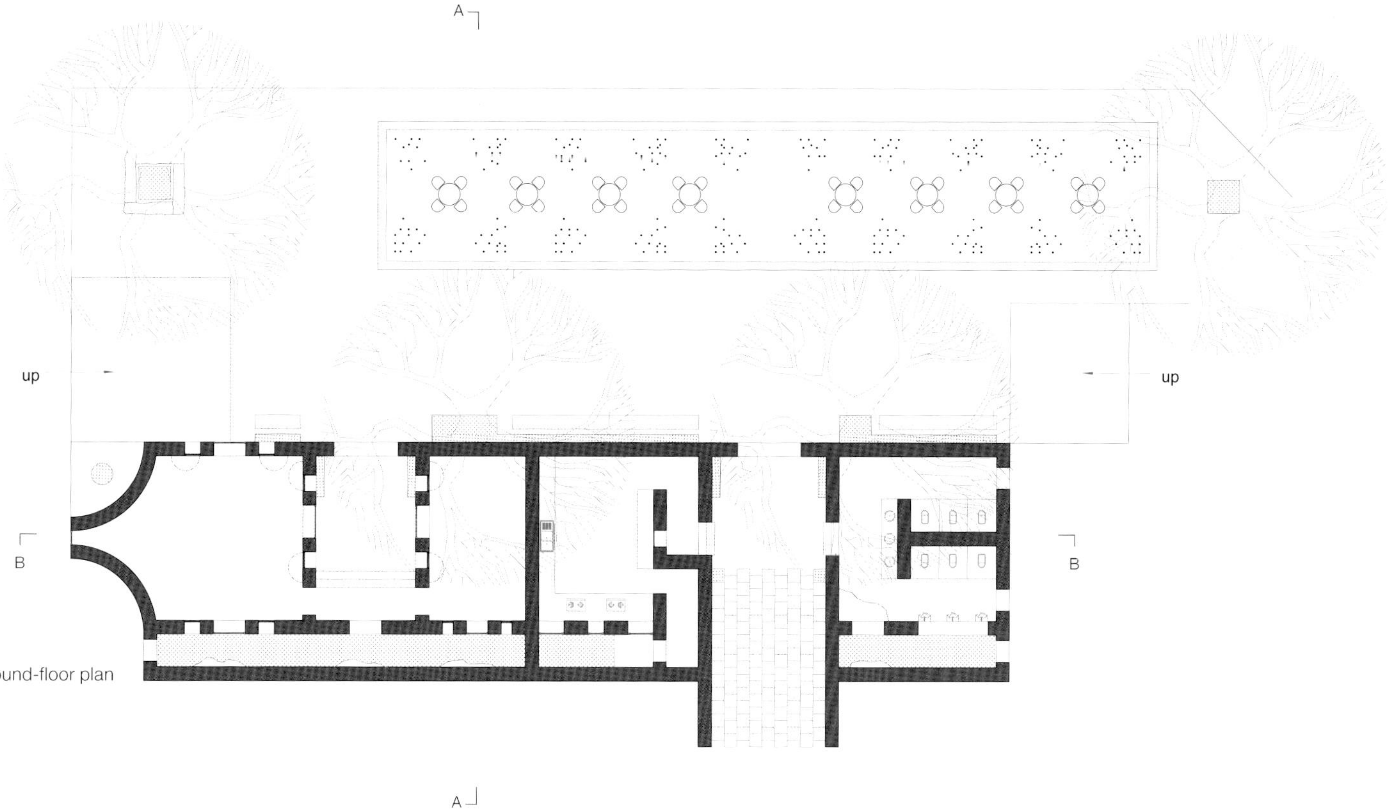

Ground-floor plan

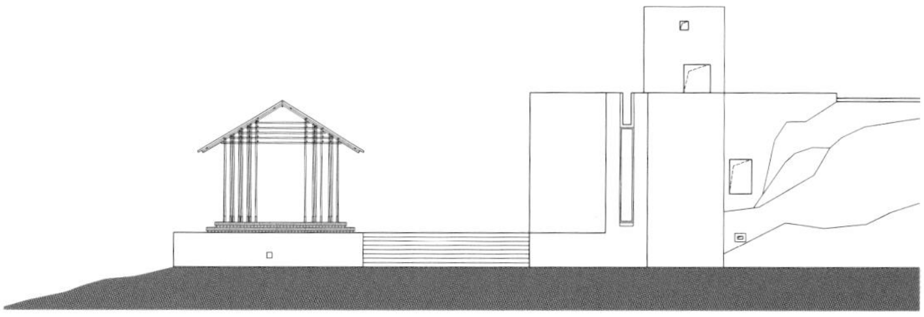
West elevation

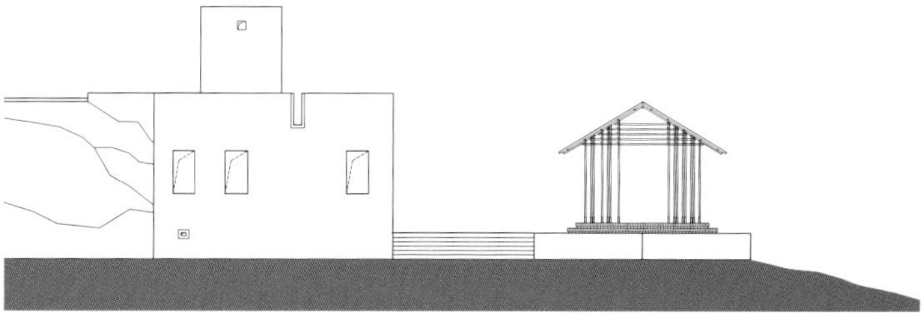
East elevation

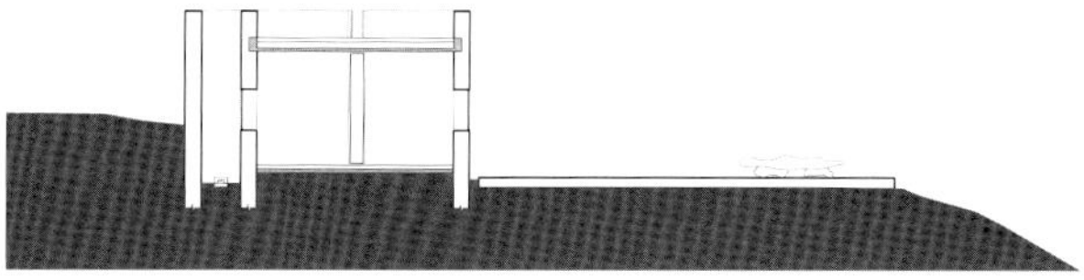
Section A-A

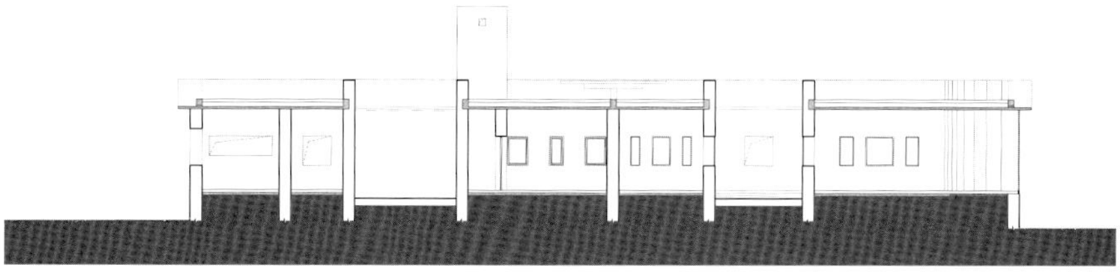
Section B-B

Huang Zhe + Huang Li + Zhang Yao

OfficeOffCourse

Founded in 2012, OfficeOffCourse is currently based in Shanghai, Hangzhou, and Boston. The core design team takes on a variety of tasks that span urban planning, architecture, landscape architecture, and interior design. They bring into their works a wealth of professional experience gathered through their time with many world-renowned architecture offices and institutes in the United States, the Netherlands, Japan, Mexico, and Spain. They have participated in a wide range of projects and share extensive architectural backgrounds, as well as practical experience. The office is engaged in a variety of projects in China, Japan, Australia, and the United States, and which include museums, private residences, office buildings, urban planning projects, historical building renovations, and schools.

OfficeOffCourse explores and extends the core values of architecture in the face of both globalization and localization. Their projects bridge history, nature, and space; discuss typologies of architecture and landscape in different contexts; and expand unknown boundaries beyond limits. Meanwhile, the studio focuses on the creative application of traditional materials through modern technology, the organic redevelopment of historical heritage, and through critiquing the diversification of contemporary cities. OfficeOffCourse's multidisciplinary collaboration at the beginning of each project comes from a systematic integration that offers innovative design solutions.

Selected Works

2015 OfficeOffCourse, Hangzhou, China
2016 123+ Growth Center, Shanghai, China
2017 Windouble Headquarter (under construction), Shanghai, China
2018 Yue Ware Museum at Shanglin Lake, Cixi, China
2018 Shadow Garden in 10th Jiangsu Horticultural Expo, Yangzhou, China
2018 Keqiao Leisure Complex (under construction), Shaoxing, China
2018 Sanlin Park Pavilions (under construction). Shanghai, China
2019 House Hisazumi, Gifu, Japan
2019 Visitor Center in Longquan Dayao National Archaeological Park, Longquan, China
2019 Exhibition Center in Longquan Dayao National Archaeological Park, Longquan, China
2019 Jiuji Gallery (under construction), Hangzhou, China

Exhibition Center in Longquan Dayao National Archaeological Park © OfficeOffCourse

House Hisazumi © OfficeOffCourse

Interviewer: Fang Ziyu
Interviewee: Huang Zhe, Huang Li, Zhang Yao (OfficeOffCourse)
Editor: Mo Wanli

What is your understanding of "building with nature?"

OfficeOffCourse: If we look at the words "nature" and "building" separately, then they're two completely different ideas. In terms of dimension and breadth, a number of disciplines have interpreted them differently at different points in history, so there's no way to expand on them individually. But the respective meanings of those terms are more precise when they're put together. Different ways of arranging the words create varying meanings, with "building nature" and "building with nature" representing two very different ideas. The former emphasizes results; the latter emphasizes a pathway. "Building with nature" is like other pathways: it needs its own core, or at least it needs to be rid of the more complete aesthetic mechanisms created by existing pathways.

From that, we understand "building with nature" as an operational method of construction that puts an emphasis on taking advantage of the given environment. You can choose to adopt it or you don't; it's not necessarily better or worse than other operational methods. With "building with nature" being just one pathway, excellence arises primarily from what you want to do, as well as from the dynamic and complex relationship between the pathway you choose and what you do.

123+ Growth Center © Office Off Course

What are the main directions that your practice is currently exploring?

OfficeOffCourse: Let us use our installation Now You See, Now You Don't to respond to the question. The project is incredibly simple from the final perception of the viewer: it's a real but abstract 3D object that disappears and reappears in front of the viewer in real time, depending on the relationship between the viewer and the environment. This phenomenon is intuitive, real, and yet, unfamiliar. Because of that, the viewer's intuition is to constantly redefine the object and its surrounding space as a spectrum of possibilities throughout the viewing process. Some see a plane, while others see an empty space. Through the entire experience, this kind of natural phenomenon creates a constant cycle of self-questioning about the object, self, and space–time.

The way we realize this abundance of impossibilities, though, is incredibly natural and simple. There's no technical control over it. We just use the inherent characteristics of a common foam material and place it at its given site using the most primitive means of construction. We simply leave it there, without any superfluous movements. The entire structure and construction follow the material in coming together, forgetting even the most basic common-sense techniques.

However, this natural way of forgetting what you've learned and seemingly doing nothing at all actually involved over a year of repeated trial-and-error, explorations, and breakthroughs. One the one hand, it is neither a linear nor simple process. On the other hand, it's also not a continuation or a questioning of existing knowledge and propositions. In this regard, we completely understand the difficulties and mindset that Junya Ishigami had in his graduation project. Although we've never met, and the content, direction, and standards of our work also differ, but our work methods have some resonance. That would be our relation to "building with nature," if we can make that connection. Likewise, we have continued to develop and deepen this method of exploration—one that's not set, and which can be perpetually explored in different directions.

VISITOR CENTER IN LONGQUAN DAYAO NATIONAL ARCHAEOLOGICAL PARK

Location: Longquan, Zhejiang, China
Architect: OfficeOffCourse
Principal architect: Huang Zhe, Huang Li, Zhang Yao
Design team: Ye Sunhui, Yu Jieying, Dong Fanzheng, Bao Liling, Bai Lu, Wu Xiumin
Structure design team: Ma Yonghua, Jiang Shuangyi
Mechanical team: Lin Li, Zhang Yuhua
Gross floor area: 950 square meters
Completion: 2019
Photography: OfficeOffCourse

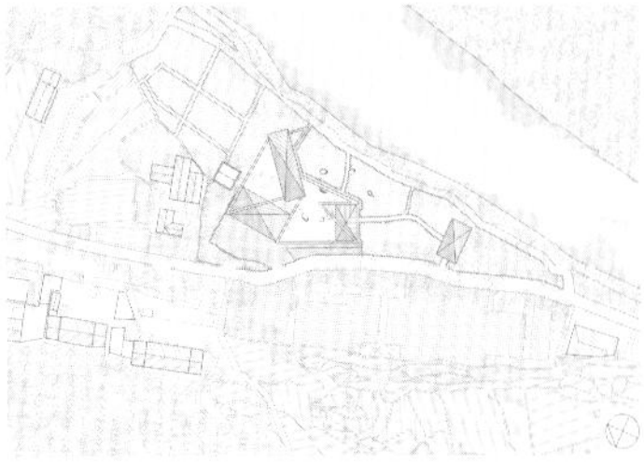

Site plan

Aerial view

Entrance to the exhbition center

Longquan celadon is a green-glazed historical Chinese ceramic known in the West as celadon or greenware. The Longquan kiln was first fired in the early Northern Song Dynasty and flourished from the Southern Song Dynasty to the early Yuan Dynasty before it was shut down after the middle of the Qing Dynasty. The collective heritage sites, which were the core production area of Longquan kiln, became a national heritage conservation in 1988, and later, a national archaeological park in 2018. The Visitor Center, as one in a group of new public buildings in the national archaeological park, is located in Jin Village, an ancient village surrounded by mountains and rivers. While its architectural style should fit with the fabric of the village, it also needs to project a symbolic significance of the national park. In this context, this project deals with the relationship between natural and manufactured, and tradition, and modern, as well as the relationship between the materials and the construction crafts.

Design Strategy

The project consists of a continuous wall, which defines the boundary of three individual buildings containing multiple functions that include exhibition, viewing, and shuttle bus boarding. This decentralized functional distribution allows each building to be small enough to live in harmony with surrounding environment. The continuous wall appears as an organizer in this scheme, connecting the three buildings. It is made up of three sets of parallel walls, which are the short sides of the three small buildings. The glass façades, which are the long sides of the three houses divide the site into five courtyards of different sizes. At the same time, the wall diagonally separates each building into rooms of different sizes. This division offers each room a strong directional property and this directional property builds a connection between the building and the site in the corresponding orientations: facing river, courtyard, parking, or entrance, depending on which suits the program of the room.

Due to the separation of the continuous wall, the buildings no longer present as a whole. However, parts in an episodic scene gain the opportunity to be read as independent buildings, since the integrity of the symbol is maintained. It makes the relationship between the wall, the building, and the courtyard closer and more complex.

Based on the episodic reading of this building, the spiral staircase and ramp leading to the second floor are placed away from the building, hiding its direct connection to the building. In this way, both of them are also read as independent elements. They are placed in the courtyard like landscape sculptures, rather than as subordinates of the main building, thus reconstructing the dialogue between the part and the whole.